W9-ASP-929

Positively
Connecticut

Diane Smith

The
Globe
Pequot
press

Old Saybrook, Connecticut

Text design by Saralyn D'Amato-Twomey
Photo on page 154 by Julie Bidwell
Photo on page 1 © C. Kirby Studio
Illustrations by Diane Blasius
Original video footage by John Roll, Ken Melech, Kort Frydenborg, Mark Ciesinski, Tim Clune, Mark Desy, George DeYounge, Tom Parent, Joe Sferrazza, R. J. Tattersall, Tim Wright
Drawing of the *Amistad* (page 54) courtesy Amistad America, Inc.

Library of Congress Cataloging-in-Publication Data Is Available
ISBN 0-7627-0340-7

Printed in Quebec, Canada
First Edition/First Printing

Contents

Acknowledgments

There are more people to thank than I could possibly name here, including all the television viewers who watch every day and make me feel part of their families. I am grateful to each of the people in these stories who opened their lives to our cameras. I keep them all in my heart.

There are so many people to thank at WTNH TV, past and present, who have made each day an adventure.

This book would not be possible without Hank Yaggi, WTNH president and general manager, who decided the best way for a TV station to celebrate its fiftieth anniversary is to celebrate its community with a book that is a lasting tribute. Thanks to Val Yaggi, who started this project innocently enough with a well-timed question at a Beach Club luncheon. Mary Lee Weber, thanks for believing.

I am grateful to Billy Otwell, Mike Sechrist, Kenn Venit, and all the other news executives who know that "good" news is important and allowed me to pursue it.

Thanks to the producers who allotted a few extra seconds to allow these stories to "breathe" on the air.

Most of all I thank all the photographers whose video made the stories, and whose unfailing good humor made the reporting fun. I especially thank John Roll, a gifted photographer and producer, who through seven years and more than 300 assignments had a fresh idea for every story. Kort Frydenborg introduced me to Connecticut Yankees. I thank Ken Melech for enduring "the Diane Smith workout" weekly as we shoot *Positively Connecticut* and for striking up the band every morning.

I greatly value the friendship and encouragement of Roxanne Coady of R. J. Julia Booksellers, who opened the doors to this project.

I am grateful to all the people at Globe Pequot who "got it" right away and then made it happen, including Linda Kennedy, Mike Urban, Kevin Lynch, Saralyn D'Amato-Twomey, Dana Baylor, and Jane Reilly. Thanks for your belief that this could be a book, and for your diligence in overcoming the hurdles. To my editor, Paula Brisco, thanks for your wisdom and your unflagging ability to "take another look."

I am most grateful to the most important people in my life, my family. My sisters and brother and their spouses listened (and listened and listened), advised, and cheered. Thanks to Mom, who reminded me to "think before you write" and enrolled me in creative writing courses instead of summer camp. I still can't hit a softball, but I learned to love language. Thanks to Dad, who taught me the art of storytelling.

To my husband, Tom Woodruff, who doesn't have the word NO in his vocabulary, I owe everything. He kept us moving, captured video images, typed copy, untangled computer troubles, and even dog wrangled. His energy and optimism and faith carry me every day.

Introduction

As a news anchor and reporter, I got tired of people saying that there's nothing but bad news on TV. Starting in 1985 I set out to discover the good news, the things that make people feel good about Connecticut. That's how *Positively Connecticut*, the weekly news segment on WTNH-TV 8, was born.

For inspiration I had Charles Kuralt, the best storyteller on television, who had criss-crossed the nation for his series *On the Road*. I have traveled the highways, byways, and waterways of this wonderful state, seeking the people and places that make our corner of New England great, that give it character and heart and tradition. Along the way, I realized that these are more than stories about New England—they are stories about America.

For several years, viewers have asked me to compile the stories into a book. Here it is! The people on these pages are some of the most memorable, but there are many more in the fascinating cast of characters that has populated *Positively Connecticut*.

In converting *Positively Connecticut*, the on-air series, into a book, we have worked hard to present the stories in a way that captures the original flavor of the TV segments. That meant preserving the original conversations with the people in the stories, as well as overcoming technical hurdles to capture images for these pages from the original video footage. Some of the stories go back more than a dozen years, but in updating them for this book, I was thrilled to learn that many of these everyday heroes are still pursuing their passions and dreams, still living lives that are positively Connecticut.

I hope this book will bring back fond memories for some of you and introduce others to the special qualities of the place we call home, Connecticut.

I'll see you on TV!

People with Passion

Excambian Labor of Love

Most TV reporters move around so much that very few ever have the opportunity to follow-up on a story that took ten years from beginning to end. That's why this is one of my favorite stories. I had the opportunity to be there near the beginning and at the end—with a decade in between. This is a story about people who cherished their work so much that even after going on to hard-earned retirement after long years in aircraft manufacture, they came back together as volunteers to do what they loved. The same people who had originally built an innovative airplane reunited to restore what they had created. And they did it with the blessing and more than a little help, from the company that had originally built the flying boat—Sikorsky.

Excambian was the flying boat that made the dream of regular flights across the Atlantic a reality, more than half a century ago. Built for airline use, during World War II it was used by the Navy to ferry VIPs. Forty years later Excambian came home to Stratford, having barely survived postwar service as a commercial transport.

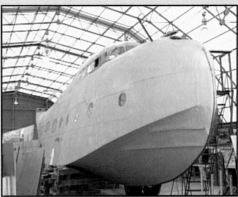

Harry Hleva was an apprentice engineer in the 1940s when Excambian was built. Here's what he said in 1987 after the airplane returned to Connecticut.

Harry: *"I cringe when I look at her now after seeing the way she was originally. She's been neglected, badly abused. Hope we can make her well."*

Hleva put together a team of volunteers to restore Excambian to her former glory. Now the restoration is finished.

Harry: *"It's been a picnic. Real fun, real nice people, great camaraderie and love for history. It's been fun."*

Diane: *"What motivates these men to work so hard?"*

Harry: *"Love of restoration, and [he chuckles] love of their families. Husband and wife weren't meant to live together twenty-four hours a day, and they learned that after they retired."*

John Liddell was the original flight engineer on Excambian. He remembered the generals and Hollywood stars who traveled on Excambian; remembered, too, being shot at on one secret mission. He recalled the early days of the restoration.

John: *"I didn't think we were going to make it when I first saw this thing when it came back from Florida. I never thought they could restore this thing to a decent museum piece. These fellas have done a fantastic job."*

Joe Losardo was retired when Excambian came home to Connecticut.

Joe: *"I did see it on the six o'clock news, and they said they were gonna restore it. And I said, 'Not without me.'"*

Losardo has spent nineteen thousand hours restoring the flying boat. He thinks the volunteer workers needed the plane as much as Excambian needed them.

Joe: *"You retire, you waste away. You gotta keep moving. It was a great ten years. You can't imagine the enjoyment we had working here."*

And it was hard work, too. Much of Excambian had to be completely rebuilt, not just restored. Sikorsky picked up the $700,000 tab.

Harry: *"We never lost faith. We knew it could be done. It was built once before, and we knew it could be done again."*

The team worked with true devotion, leaving a piece of themselves for history.

John Liddell: *"A lot of us feel that it's our last big project. I mean, after this is finished, we'll probably go back and pat it and look at it."*

Excambian's final journey is to the New England Air Museum in Windsor Locks. It's about seventy-one miles from the hangar in Stratford, and since the plane will never fly again, it's going by truck, with a special escort of state police.

When Excambian pulls out, you can bet this crew will be here to say good-bye.

Joe Losardo (his voice breaking a little): *"That's gonna be a sad day. It really bothers me to see that it's gonna go away."*

Harry Hleva: *"I think we'll all smile at it and say 'Job well done.' We'll all go home with a nice smile on our faces and a warm feeling that we've done something real good."*

Something really good, that's positively Connecticut. 🖊

P.S.:

_____

Excambian can now be toured at the New England Air Museum in Windsor Locks.

The Abbey

*S*even times each day and once in the middle of the night, the bell calls the nuns to prayer at the Abbey of Regina Laudis. Their prayer is in Latin and in song. It's the ancient Gregorian chant. These Benedictine sisters are believed to be the only community of women in the United States devoted to the chant.

Mother Margaret Georgina Patton describes the importance of chant in the cloistered life of this monastery, founded fifty years ago by Lady Abbess Benedict Duss (portrayed by Loretta Young in the film *Come to the Stable*).

Mother Margaret Georgina: *"I can't imagine living this life without chant. It's that sustaining to me. For all of us the fact that it punctuates the day means a lot and changes our lives."*

At the end of World War II, Lady Abbess, an American nun, left France to open an abbey in Bethlehem, Connecticut, in tribute to General George Patton who liberated her Nazi-occupied monastery. Mother Margaret Georgina is the general's granddaughter and one of forty women who now live behind the walls of the abbey in a nearly self-sufficient community. There is a working farm on the abbey's 350 acres. Cows provide

7

milk and cheese; sheep provide wool for sweaters.

Each nun is devoted to one discipline or task. After entering the abbey, Mother Margaret Georgina went back to school to earn a degree in horticulture.

Mother Margaret Georgina: *"We are all obligated for this land, and I'm glad to be able to play my part by having learned to grow flowers."*

There is much beauty here. Mother Praxedes is the resident artist. Her sculptures dot the landscape and are incorporated into the new church—the church the nuns designed together.

The church reflects the Benedictine principles of stewardship of the land. Glass walls allow the outside to come inside.

Mother Praxedes: *"The land informs our prayer, and our prayer informs the way we work on the land."*

Prayer guides the nuns' lives, whether they are working their farm, tending their forest preserve, or operating their blacksmith shop, where Mother Anastasia dons a blue denim habit.

Mother Anastasia: *"We do all kinds of things. . . . It's wonderful because if somebody has a need in the house, you don't always have to go down to the hardware store."*

The blacksmith shop is where they made the iron grill that separates the nuns from the people who attend vespers in their church. The grill is a metaphor for their lives, separating them from the world, yet permeable. For although the nuns

live in what they call "enclosures," they also interact with the world. As Benedictines they are commanded to offer hospitality to those seeking spirituality.

Sister Lioba recalls her first visit.

Sister Lioba: *"A friend of mine said you'll love it. And I*

said, oh well . . . a monastery . . . I don't know."

But she returned.

Sister Lioba: *"I was seeking some kind of truth and some kind of integrity, and I found it here. It was the strength of the sisters, the integrity of their dedication to the land, their professionalism—all of those things spoke to me as a modern woman."*

Yes, these are modern women, with careers in law, chemistry, agriculture, medicine, literature, and art, living a monastic life with roots in the sixth century.

Sister Ozanne grew up in Wethersfield.

Sister Ozanne: *"I saw these women truly landed and grounded, and through the land knowing themselves and one another and knowing God."*

The women agreed to record a CD of their chants because of their sense that people are searching for spiritual awakening.

Mother Margaret Georgina: *"We sing for the world. . . . If people are looking for something, and we can offer it, then that's an extension of our Benedictine hospitality."*

A hospitality infused with faith that is positively Connecticut. 🍃

A LITTLE MORE:

The original plan was to sell the CD, Women in Chant, *in the shop at the abbey, but in the first month the CD was available, it sold out its three thousand copies. That's when a record label from Colorado heard about it, and now the CD is available nationwide.*

Salt and Pepper

NEW HAVEN

They practice in a black Episcopal church in the predominantly black neighborhood of Newhallville in New Haven. But the members of the Salt and Pepper Singers are black and white, from inner city and suburbs. They are janitors, lawyers, factory workers, even a poet. They come together in the love of gospel music.

The Salt and Pepper Singers are the brain-child of Mae Gibson Brown and Sheila Bonenberger. Sheila heard Mae and her children sing at a potluck supper at a school in Branford and asked if they could try singing together.

Sheila remembers being impressed and moved by Mae and her children.

Sheila: *"It was more than a vocal blend, more than technical perfection, it was a spirit, a kind of a glue that held their voices together. It was a unity of purpose, of spirit, I guess maybe of love."*

You feel that in Salt and Pepper. The driving force is its director, twenty-three-year-old Chuck Brown, Mae's son.

Chuck: *"I want Salt and Pepper to not be a black-sounding gospel choir. I want it to be that perfect mixture of the angelic quality that comes from the salts and the soulful quality that comes from the peppers."*

Chuck is energetic and highly animated as he leads the choir in rehearsal. He urges the choir to use more staccato as it sings the words "My Father's wish."

Choir: *"My Father's wish . . ."*

Chuck: *"Sopranos now, He holds the power of the world, in His hands... "*

Choir (clapping): *"Power of the world, in His hands ... power of the world, in His hands ..."*

An actor, dancer, and singer with a six-octave range, Chuck is also a spirited leader.

Chuck: *"We demand good intentions, we demand communication, and I demand love."*

The singers are of all denominations, some are Jewish, some even call themselves atheists. But Mae sees their performances as a ministry.

Mae: *"When we've gone into convalescent homes, or into prisons, or into shelters, it's a message of hope, to say that this is the situation now, but it not necessarily will be this way always for you."*

Choir: *"He loves us, and He cares so much, He wants us to be His very own."*

Singing, swaying, and clapping, the choir voices words of hope.

Choir: *"We shall be as one ... we shall be as one ... we shall be as one someday."*

Mae: *"I think in an ideal world, we hope that would be the situation in every church and in every group that would get together, that it would be a salt and pepper group, that it would not be totally all black or totally all white. But until that happens we are enjoying sharing what we do together."*

Choir: *"We shall overcome, we shall overcome, we shall overcome some day."*

To hear Salt and Pepper sing those lyrics is to truly feel their meaning, and to wonder what we could accomplish in a truly integrated world. That's the spirit of Salt and Pepper, a spirit that's positively Connecticut. 🎵

SINCE OUR STORY:

Salt and Pepper will soon celebrate its fifteenth anniversary. The choir is the subject of a documentary on the healing power of gospel music, called Not Just Good Time Sunday, *which was shown at the Cannes Film Festival and is in the permanent archives of the Museum of Modern Art. In that film Mae says, "We pray that when we sing, the people that are there will not leave the same way they came, but will take something away with them." One member of an all-white audience says after the performance, "It broke down barriers just watching them."*

Salt and Pepper is now directed by Ron Pollard. Their charismatic former leader, Charles C. C. Brown, is still on the board of directors. And he is now performing in Broadway musicals such as Dreamgirls, Miss Saigon, *and* Rent.

The Hendersons in Silo Country

NEW MILFORD

There's a spot in Litchfield County known to local people as Silo Country. For the past twenty-five years, the "mayor" and "first lady" there have been two rather unlikely farmers, Skitch and Ruth Henderson.

When New York Pops conductor Skitch Henderson takes a break from the concert hall, he leaves his white tie and tails behind, in favor of blue jeans and his tractor at his Hunt Hill Farm in New Milford.

Skitch: *"When I first came up here, there was no one here but Arthur Miller and myself. By that I mean no one in our business. We would get together and talk about fuel oil for tractors, and the farmers would look at us like we were from Mars."*

By "our business" Skitch means show business. Miller, the playwright, and Henderson, the music director of NBC, were looking for some country solitude. But it was Henderson's wife, Ruth, who discovered Hunt Hill Farm nearly thirty years ago.

Ruth: *"I just loved it! It reminded me of Germany, strangely enough. My part of Germany where I come from, and especially the barnyard."*

In the barnyard these days, the animals are abstract wood sculpture by a local artist.

P.S.:

Although the Hendersons travel worldwide to accommodate Skitch's concert schedule, they consider New Milford home and are very committed to the community. Each year at the holidays they hold a fundraiser for New Milford Hospital at their home. Guests bid on mystery packages donated by area celebrities like Whoopi Goldberg. One recent party raised $25,000 for the hospital.

Inside the barn is a show featuring another local artist, book illustrator Wendell Minor.

The farm is more than the Hendersons' country retreat. In 1972 Ruth opened The Silo, a gourmet shop, cooking school, and art gallery.

Ruth: *"At that time we already had a restaurant in New York. My first little store here, I only bought from the restaurant district because that's what I knew about, and people were absolutely intrigued."*

The Silo regularly offers classes with renowned chefs. The two cookbooks written by Skitch and Ruth capture the essence of the Hendersons' country lifestyle. At The Silo, you might even find Skitch himself, making his daughter-in-law's bread pudding.

Skitch: *"Always use your hands, it makes it taste better."*

Diane: *"When you leave the concert hall, you're thinking about the country and that tractor, aren't you?"*

Skitch: *"I love the tractor, I love the trucks, I love my neighbor Bud. I love the dogs, cats, the fields, the weeds, the headaches, the snow, rain, and mud."*

Diane: *"At some point you'll be able to leave this to another generation and hopefully they will love it and preserve it also."*

Skitch: *"I hope they'll enjoy it. Because it's Valhalla to me."*

And positively Connecticut to us. 🍃

King of Collectibles

WEST HARTFORD

A newspaper columnist once wrote, "Mickey Mantle may be the king of modern-day sports collectibles, but Neil Sakow is the keeper of the kingdom." The keeper is a one-of-a-kind figure.

"Attention please, ladies and gentlemen: now arriving at the American Dream today from Channel 8—Diane Smith!"

Being greeted by Neil Sakow at his American Dream Museum is a little like being introduced at Yankee Stadium.

Neil: "In this museum dedicated to the icons of my childhood, Mickey Mantle is playing centerfield every day, the Yankees are the best team in baseball, Howdy Doody is the number-one children's television show in America, and John Fitzgerald Kennedy is president of these United States."

We'd all have great collectibles worth big bucks, if not for moms who cleaned out childhood toy boxes, but it seems Neil's mother never threw anything out. That's why he has a baseball card identical to one that recently sold at Sotheby's for $49,000, as well as Kennedy memorabilia from his dad's five-and-ten-cent store.

Neil: "This is a bubble gum cigar with 'Win with Jack' on the box. We had them in our store when I was a kid in 1960. We put a box of

Kennedy cigars and a box of Nixon cigars side by side, and Kennedy won hands down."

Neil's jukebox plays Sinatra singing JFK's campaign song, "High Hopes," and Neil sings along:

"K-e-double-n-e-d-y,
Jack's the nation's favorite guy.
Everyone wants to back Jack."

Neil: *"That's how that went with Frank Sinatra, but I think I sing it better."*

His three-story apartment building in West Hartford is overflowing with memorabilia. That forty-year-old bottle of Howdy Doody grape juice is worth over $200 now, and there's an unopened jar of Hopalong Cassidy peanut butter.

Neil: *"And anybody that messes with me, I take out my Roy Rogers holsters in the original box."* He points his Roy Rogers six-shooter at me.

Neil shows his collection by appointment only. And if he really likes you, he may take you upstairs.

Neil: *"When you think you've seen it all, I show you this: the Howdy Doody Room."*

He spreads his arms wide with glee and launches into the Howdy Doody theme song.

"I'm for Howdy Doody . . . are you? Yes I am!"

How did he know what to start collecting at the age of six? Neil says he's clairvoyant. He seems like a time traveler who

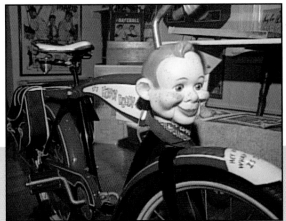

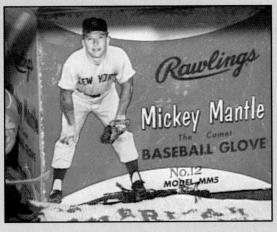

SINCE OUR STORY:

The great Mickey Mantle has passed away , and the value of Mantle memorabilia has skyrocketed. That's why Neil says fervently: "Every day I feel like I've gone to heaven when I look at my collection of the great number seven."

Neil is considering moving his collection to Branson, Missouri, but he's still located in West Hartford for now. The new third floor of the American Dream Museum is devoted to "one-of-a-kind pop culture items from the forties, fifties, and a few from the sixties." What qualifies? A Desi Arnaz conga drum and a Pee Wee Reese marbles game, to name two items. Neil celebrated the fiftieth anniversary of the first broadcast of his favorite TV show by publishing his fourth book, Living in a Howdy Doody World. *That's in addition to* The Most Mickeys on My Mantle, Still More Mickeys on My Mantle, *and* Unbelievably Still More Mickeys on My Mantle.

Neil's favorite description of himself comes from a newspaper reporter who described him as a "sugared-up twelve-year-old in a forty-something body." His philosophy on the art of collecting: "Old is gold."

discovered what would be valuable in the 1990s, then went back forty years to get it.

Neil: *"When I would come home from school, I would work on my baseball card collection and my scrapbooks and I didn't do too much homework. But I guess as the way things worked out, thank you very much, it worked out all right."* He laughs.

Neil has spent a lifetime collecting, and making money at it, too. Although he seems as boyish as Peter Pan's brother, his devotion to collecting has made him the man with the *Most Mickeys on my Mantle,* as he titled his first book. "I Love Mickey" (a pop song written and sung by Teresa Brewer) reverberates through his home and his life.

Neil leaves us with a thought that summarizes his joyful outlook: *"It's unreal Neil appeal with all the zeal and that's my schpiel."*

And that's positively Connecticut!

Witch's Dungeon

BRISTOL

I had heard about Cortlandt Hull and his Witch's Dungeon for years. I'd heard the scary display rivaled the quality you'd see at major theme parks based on Hollywood movie studios. So one Halloween, when I went to meet Cortlandt and visit his dungeon, I got a shock I never expected: The display was crammed into a little building that looks like somebody's tool shed. But step through the door, into the darkness, and you lose the sense that you are inside a tiny building. Then the real shocks begin.

Cortlandt opens the dungeon for only a few days annually around Halloween, but he works on the display year-round. The mystery to me is that he's still here in Bristol and not in Hollywood.

It all started when Cortlandt Hull was just seven years old and saw the classic film *Frankenstein*. He was hooked on horror.

Cortlandt: *"So I collected the posters, the lobby cards, the little model kits that came out in the sixties, but it wasn't enough for me. I wanted full-size, three-dimensional, life-size figures."*

So he started building them.

Cortlandt: *"It's like any other hobby, only*

this one is like Frankenstein's monster. It got out of control."

At thirteen, Cortlandt constructed the Witch's Dungeon behind his house to exhibit his monsters. Enter, and you are greeted by a skeleton sounding just like Vincent Price.

Skeleton: *"Welcome, poor mortal, to this witch's dungeon of nightmares."*

Inside, Frankenstein's monster lurks in the semi-darkness, a creature looking exactly as Boris Karloff played him in the movie.

A warning voice is heard: "You have created a monster, and it will destroy you."

Cortlandt: *"I wanted to capture something about the gauntness that Karloff had in his face at the time. He had taken out some bridges in his teeth and that made him look even more gaunt."*

Cortlandt's models are a tribute to the classic horror films—the ones that made hideous monsters into American icons. Each scene is like a frame of film, blown

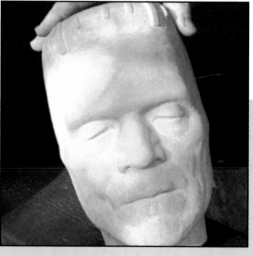

up into three terrifying dimensions.

The lights dim, and when they come up again, Kharis the Mummy confronts us.

Another warning voice speaks: *"Kharis still lives."*

Cortlandt describes the scene: *"It's like a moment frozen in time when he pushes the lid aside and is coming out."*

The startling likenesses are due in part to Cortlandt's skill as a professional artist and in part to friendships with Hollywood movie greats who have helped him get access to the tools of the trade—like the life casts made from Boris Karloff's face and the original molds used to make the creature for *Creature from the Black Lagoon*.

There are more touches that movie buffs will relish. Like the crest on Dracula's wall, taken from the ring Bela Lugosi wore in the film—the ring Cortlandt now wears.

Several years ago a real monster surfaced. A lawyer for Universal Pictures tried to shut the Witch's Dungeon down unless Hull paid for use of the characters. It was a price Cortlandt could not afford from his admission fee of only 50 cents.

But actor Vincent Price and others rallied to the dungeon's defense against Universal.

Cortlandt: *"Vincent, as a matter of fact, stated that it was disgraceful and unworthy of a great company."*

When the people at Universal learned the dungeon measures only eight by twenty feet, and is open only for Halloween, they backed off. This is now the only seasonal display endorsed not only by the movie studio, but also by the offspring of the actors who made the monsters famous.

Cortlandt: *"The enjoyment people get from this—that's why I do it year after year."*

Year after year, for thirty years. The Witch's Dungeon, a Halloween tradition that's positively Connecticut. ☙

A FINAL WORD:

The people who line up every year to enter the Witch's Dungeon appreciate Cortlandt and his creations. So do the people in Hollywood, the people he pays tribute to. When Cortlandt was in trouble, they rallied to his defense because the actors who had portrayed the monsters, and the actors' children, are his friends. If you're lucky, your 50 cents will buy you admission to the dungeon and a chance to meet Boris Karloff's daughter or Lon Chaney's grandson. They've been known to make the pilgrimage to Bristol, too.

Lincoln's Detective

NORTH HAVEN

"You'll hate me if I say this…" "Oh come on, Joe, go ahead, say what?" "Well, okay … (long pause) I don't really do it for the money. I do it because it's a thrill to find these treasures and hold them in my hands."

That's the conversation I had with Joe Buberger. And I believe him. What treasures? How about the first known photo of President Lincoln? Buberger is a former cop, forced to retire at thirty after a taxi slammed into his patrol car, causing lasting hip problems. But like a good cop, he is still searching for clues and solving mysteries, only now the mysteries are in the images of history.

Is your image of Abraham Lincoln the face on the five-dollar bill?

Or the distinguished and careworn president captured on film by renowned Civil War photographer Matthew Brady?

Or Henry Fonda in the 1940 film *Young Mr. Lincoln?*

Would you believe this photo may be the earliest known image of Lincoln, taken when he was in his early thirties? It's a daguerreotype, an early form of photography. Its new owners, a couple by the name of Hoffman, set out to discover if it is authentic.

Joe Buberger: *"They showed it to one curator, and he looked at it, and he handed it back to them and said, 'This is not Lincoln; it has no presence.'"*

But another expert disagreed, so the Hoffmans enlisted Buberger. The ex-New Haven cop now uses his forensic skills to authenticate old daguerreotypes and photos. He recalls the moment he first saw this one.

Joe: *"I tried to be cool, but I was happy I was sitting down when they handed it to me. I was really just stunned."*

But Lincoln expert Lloyd Ostendorf was skeptical.

Joe: *"He flat out said no, it wasn't Lincoln. So that made my battle a lot tougher for the last few years."*

Buberger says Ostendorf defied the evidence, acting like the early astronomers who thought they had seen it all and were ready to say, 'Throw away the telescope, there are no more stars.'

Joe: *"He just couldn't accept it was happening . . . that somebody discovered another galaxy."*

Buberger sought out a photo researcher in Coventry, who created an image overlay that seemed to match other Lincoln photos. Then he contacted Henry Lee, director of the state's forensic crime lab, who sent him to a forensic anthropologist. This scientist compared the photo with what was known about Honest Abe's face—everything from the shape of the lips to indentations in the ear—and pronounced it . . . Lincoln. Two more biomedical people agreed, including a professor whose computer searched thousands of faces in its data bank and matched the Hoffman's daguerreotype with Lincoln.

Buberger was becoming more and more sure of the finding.

Joe: *"I guess only his mother could say, 'Yep, that's my Abie,'"* he says in his dry manner, with more than a touch of his boyhood Brooklyn in his humor and accent. But it was all looking very good.

The final piece to the puzzle was found by a historian who traced the daguerreotype to a drawer in a desk in the home of a descendant of Lincoln's personal secretary. Buberger was convinced, and elated.

Joe: *"I feel very fortunate that I happened to be able to hold Lincoln in my hands. It's something that I think eventually the whole world's gonna know about."*

And when it does, they'll have to credit Joe Buberger for a contribution to history that's positively Connecticut. 🎷

UPDATE:

That daguerreotype is still in the Hoffmans' private collection. Buberger estimates it could be worth as much as $20 million. Recently he came across a photo that excited him nearly as much—a previously unknown image of Vincent van Gogh, perhaps the one the artist used when creating his famous self-portraits. The photo appears to date to 1889, about a year before van Gogh killed himself.

Nuts

T he Victorian mansion in Old Lyme that hous- es the Nut Museum is showing its age, but not so its curator, Elizabeth Tashjian. Her enthusiasm for what most of us consider just a snack food is obvious from the moment one enters and pays the admission. Adults: three dollars and one nut.

Tashjian's Nut Museum, quite possibly the only one in the world, includes Elizabeth Tashjian's own paintings and sculptures of nuts, along with the world's biggest nut (a thirty-five-pound coco-de-mer) a collection of nut toys, nut jewelry, even nutcrackers. In the parlor, a nut as big as a football rests on a dainty antique chair. Coconuts, walnuts, cashews, filberts, acorns, chestnuts—they all have a place in her beloved seed collection.

Elizabeth has her own viewpoint on nut-crackers.

Elizabeth: *"Traditionally it is considered the enemy, but here through paintings and the collection we are challenging that viewpoint, and saying that nuts and nutcrackers can live in harmony."*

Living in harmony is the theme of the museum. Tashjian is aware that there is a double meaning of the word "nuts" and that

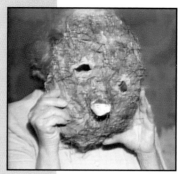

it is applied, with some lack of charity, to certain people.

Elizabeth: *"A man attempted to donate his wife for admission to the museum. That was my first clue that the word 'nut' has a good and bad connotation. In the wake of that experience I changed the purpose of the museum to a higher one, to a more humanitarian purpose."*

Tashjian says nuts have taught her about life.

Elizabeth: *"I've learned respect and gentleness from the nut, which is hard on the outside but soft and sweet on the inside."*

And she passes these lessons along to her visitors.

Four-year-old Patrick Looney (Old Lyme): *"Nuts are real nice things, not just ordinary things. They're nuts, and they're real nice."*

The symbol of the Nut Museum stands outside: a nutcracker standing over eight feet tall. When you arrive it's very important to pay attention to this nutcracker because if a pecan is hanging from it, the museum is open, and you can come right in.

Inside you may find Elizabeth singing "The Nut Anthem," which she composed. Or she may be quizzing children wearing nut masks about nutty facts.

Elizabeth: *"It takes all of humor and all of courage and all of humility to be the curator of a nut museum."*

Elizabeth Tashjian has what it takes to run the Nut Museum, an unusual institution that's positively Connecticut.

A LITTLE MORE:

Elizabeth Tashjian has been the darling of the talk show circuit, appearing frequently on the Tonight Show *and the* David Letterman Show. *During those appearances she often sings one of her original songs, with lyrics like "Nuts can be so beautiful if looked at right," or "Nuts, they've been nourishing man, ever since creation began."*

The museum faced a squirrel invasion at one point, but the Nut Lady claims that problem is a thing of the past, now that the building has a new roof. But she says, "the squirrels grabbed enough nuts to start a museum of their own."

Elizabeth is featured on the Internet at www.roadsideamerica.com/nut, with a glimpse of her nut art, snippets of her nut songs, and such quotable quotes as "Nuts are fresh tokens of primeval existence."

Ringers

DEEP RIVER

President Bush may have brought horseshoes back into fashion, but we found out that in Deep River, it never went out of style. You might call it the horseshoe-playing capital of Connecticut.

The sleepy solitude of a summer evening in Deep River ...

But on Thursday night the silence is shattered ... by iron slamming into stakes.

Horseshoes. It's a game as American as apple pie, although it was actually played by the Romans. In Deep River they've been playing every Thursday night in the spring and summer for more than forty years. John Ely is the last surviving charter member of the Pearson-Sokolowski Horseshoe League.

John Ely: *"I was new to town in Deep River and my postman, the guy that delivered the mail, was Al Pearson, and he was the founder of the league, and he asked me, 'Why don't you come up and pitch horseshoes?' So I decided I'd come, and I've been pitching ever since."*

The game's a great equalizer. Doctors, truck drivers, engineers, salesmen, Electric Boat workers—all teammates. These days a lot of the regulars are retired from their jobs, but they never miss their night of horseshoes.

John Ely: *"If you have a demanding schedule, you tell people never to plan anything for Thursday night because it's horseshoe night."*

It's a game of inches . . . or less.

Neil Johnson, league president, points to one of two shoes that are overlapping near the stake.

Neil: *"This shoe is not a point. It must show on the inside of the shoe to be a point. And there's no two points for leaners. That's just one point."*

Each ringer—with the U-shaped opening of the horseshoe hugging the stake—is worth three points.

They play the game in innings, like baseball. And like baseball, there are many different pitching styles.

Neil: *"Victor throws a one-and-three-quarter turn as it goes on. Lars is just a three-quarter."*

Then there are the eccentric styles.

Neil: *"Usually John has total disregard for the method of shooting. The shoe hits up here, it changes direction about twenty times, and it manages to get on the stake. He always says 'clean living.'"*

And how's this for clean living? (The crowd cheers as Diane pitches and makes a ringer, through the magic of TV editing.)

The world has changed a lot in the past four decades, but not horseshoes.

John Ely: *"We kind of pride ourselves on that."*

Well, maybe it has changed a little. They now total averages and handicaps by computer. But there's one thing you can bet won't change. If it's summer, and it's Thursday, in Deep River it's horseshoes, and it's positively Connecticut. ❧

17,000 Miles in a 25-Foot Boat

NEW LONDON

D avid Hays is the kind of man who dreams large dreams and then makes them come true. He did it as the founding artistic director of the National Theater of the Deaf, inventing a stage troupe consisting mostly of deaf actors who wow hearing audiences around the world. He did it again when he and his son became the first Americans to sail around Cape Horn in a boat less than thirty feet long.

On a cluster of rocks they loosely call an island, at the mouth of the Thames River in New London, is the wonderful cottage David and Daniel Hays built. It is where the father and son hatched their dream to build and sail a small boat from Connecticut to Cape Horn, at the tip of South America.

David: *"When I grew up, knowing that Cape Horn was the ultimate, I knew sailors who went around it under sail. Old men, when I was a child. The sea here has been so kind to me all my life. I felt I owed it to the sea."*

Dan was just out of college, and looking for a way to delay starting a career. Together they built *Sparrow*, a twenty-five-foot sailboat.

Diane: *"Why a twenty-five-foot boat? Why not something bigger?"*

David: *"Couldn't afford it, for one thing, and it was the perfect boat. It's perfect for two people."*

Daniel: *"When you go aground, you can jump over the side and push it off."*

Sparrow had no engine, and no sophisticated navigation gear. Their intent—to sail by the stars.

In July, Daniel set out alone.

Daniel: *"I had no idea where I was for the first two weeks. [He points to where the Thames joins Long Island Sound.] I headed out that way. I kept that lighthouse to the left and then I started going to the right and I just stayed to the right, basically. Since the wind was against me, I was always tacking into the wind. So I just kind of kept the U.S. on the right."*

David met Dan weeks later in the Caribbean for a sail that took them for an adventure through the Panama Canal, to the Galapagos Islands, and on to Easter Island, where Dan collected chunks of lava.

Then, with Cape Horn nearly in sight, a gale came up and a wall of water knocked the boat on its side.

David reads from the book they wrote about their trip. *"At 8:39 I was below, making tea and lighting the evening lamp when Sparrow went down hard to starboard. Then bam! down to port. Without a horizon below, hanging on and standing not upright but with the angle of the boat, I only knew that we were down because the water covering the port hole was not wave froth but solid green—I was looking straight down into the ocean. The water roared, like a train running over us."*

David remembers calling out:

" 'You OK, Dan?' 'I'm fine' came the answer from the deck. But his voice sounded subdued. I didn't learn until the next day that Dan had gone overboard."

Because of the danger, the sailors had told no one of their plan to round Cape Horn.

But David's wife, Leonora, trusted in them, and in the sea.

David: *"She says, 'I knew you'd come back because you were with each other.' "*

David and Dan Hays found more than adventure in that 17,000-mile trip. They found each other. Along the way, a father found a hero in his son.

They call their book *My Old Man and The Sea.*

It tells a tale that's positively Connecticut. ♪

A LITTLE MORE ABOUT THIS STORY:

Some people have beach cottages, but few have homes as whimsical as the sort of Victorian, sort of Japanese confection that David and Daniel Hays built in the mouth of the Thames River. David's extensive background in theater convinced him that building the cottage shouldn't be much more complicated than constructing a stage set. So that's what he did, designing and building it in sections at the theater center nearby. Then he and volunteers from the theater company took the sections and rowed them from shore to the island in dinghies, piecing the cottage together on the rocks. Today it's nearly as much a landmark as the lighthouse.

Bright Ideas

A Gem of a Vineyard

CLINTON

If the sun reflecting off the grapes reminds you of sparkling emeralds, you're in the right place. Chamard Vineyards is the dream come true of a man who knows a thing or two about gems. Bill Chaney started Chamard the same year that he was chairman of Tiffany's and put together a team of investors to make a leveraged buyout of the company.

Bill Chaney's transformation into a winegrower took some time.

Bill: *"It wasn't a sudden occurrence. Actually it was an evolution, enjoying fine wine, and having an appreciation for it, and loving this area, which I've known and where I've had a home for many years."*

Bill says farming is in his blood. He's the grandson of a Kansas wheat farmer. Research told him a Clinton farm, just two miles from Long Island Sound, would be a good place to make wine.

So he bought the forty-two-acre farm, which had been abandoned and overgrown. He planted grapevines, mostly Chardonnay and some red wine grapes: Pinot Noir, Merlot, and cabernet.

Bill: *"The climate is certainly right and proper. It's quite comparable to some of the finest wine regions in France."*

LOOKING AHEAD:

Ever since 60 Minutes aired a piece on the supposed health benefits of red wine, sales have been skyrocketing, and that's good for Chamard Vineyards. People are praising its Merlots and cabernets. The Pinot Noir and cabernet Franc is made in limited quantity and available only at the winery. The winery is open to visitors year-round, Wednesdays through Saturdays from 11:00 A.M. to 4:00 P.M.

Winemaker Larry McCulloch is upbeat about the Connecticut wine industry. New wineries are coming on line, and Larry says it seems that consumer acceptance of locally produced wines has turned a corner. The only problem is a shortage of locally grown grapes, and McCulloch says some landowners and farmers have approached Chamard about growing grapes for the winery.

That's why Bill hired Larry McCulloch to produce wine that would be similar in style to French wines.

Larry: *"Its subtle fruit, nice crisp acidity, and a touch of oak that we add to it makes it complex, as opposed to a California or an Australian wine with its big, massive fruit."*

The first vintage was 1988. Larry sees changes in the wine with each year's harvest.

Larry: *"Each summer is so much different, that each wine has its own quality because of the season we're having."*

The qualities of each vintage are partly decided by the weather: cool or sunny or rainy.

Diane: *"Where is the wine actually made, if you will?"*

Larry: *"In the vineyard. As a fruit grower, I know that if my crops are clean and everything is ripe, then I have to do less in the winery. I guess we like to be referred to as winegrowers, not wine makers."*

And the wine they are making is starting to draw acclaim from experts who say Connecticut wine may finally be coming into its own.

Chamard Vineyards, a gem of a winery that's positively Connecticut. 🥂

The Book Barn

When you think of buying a book, do you think of the shopping mall superstore, filled with the latest best sellers? In Bethany, book lovers think of an old red barn, with a spotted goat in a pen outside peering over a fence. It's Whitlock Book Barn, where books can sell for anything from 25 cents to $10,000.

Many years ago the barns at the Whitlock farm in Bethany sheltered sheep and turkeys.

Gilbert Whitlock: *"After the war [World War II], farming became impossible. You couldn't get help, and feed was so expensive."*

The only other business he knew was books, a business his father had been in. Gilbert kept farming, but he and his brother Everett started selling a few books at their produce stand.

Everett Whitlock: *"We had orange crates with books piled up inside. It was self-service. We left change in a box, but eventually people helped themselves to the change and we had to give it up."*

Soon the barns were brimming with books. Stephen Kobasa has been browsing here since he was a child. Now he brings his own son with him, a boy so small he can barely see into the stacks.

Stephen: *"In the old barn the books were*

just heaped up everywhere, and the sense of surprise that you got from coming across something that you hadn't known existed was, even when I was young, quite remarkable. I actually bemoaned it a little when it moved to the new facility. Everything is much more orderly and it didn't present the same kind of challenge."

Today fifty thousand used volumes are stacked on the groaning shelves. In one barn no book costs most than five dollars, and some go for as little as a quarter.

Elaine Sargent and Diane stroll through the stacks. Diane picks up a slim volume called *The Devil's Dictionary of Ambrose Bierce.*

Diane: *"This book was in my house. I thought my dad had the only copy."*

Elaine points to a shelf of books with many different titles, but matching bindings.

Elaine: *"These are books that were given to the GIs overseas during the Second World War, and now many people are interested in collecting them."*

Upstairs the Whitlocks' niece Gail Specht presides over the print loft, filled with thousands of prints and old maps from all over. Gail supervises a brisk mail-order business all over the U.S.

The other barn houses rare and antique books. There's one published in 1639, in Latin. A handwritten cookbook from 1707 not only offers recipes, but also remedies, including one for preventing plague. A book on favorite pastimes in England includes a chapter on swashbuckling. Books on fly fishing have flies that were hand-tied in the 1870s mounted on pages inside.

The Whitlocks are always buying books, by the boxful. As for the rarer vintages, they keep a "want list" at the desk. It's four pages long and includes everything from books on magic and on woodcarving to old railroad timetables.

Whitlock Book Barn. A place to uncover treasures that's positively Connecticut.

EPILOGUE:

Hard to say exactly when the Whitlocks began the Book Barn. It opened to the public in 1950, but before that there were mail-order sales. Everett had his own book business in New Haven, and in 1957 they merged into a single operation on Gilbert's farm in Bethany. They are still buying and selling books every day. Their most expensive books cost about $10,000, though the downturn in the Japanese economy in 1997 cut into sales of high-end books a bit. Neither Gilbert nor Everett has any plan to retire. Everett tells me, "I guess we'll stay here as long as the building holds up."

School on the Sound

BRIDGEPORT

As Connecticut struggles to desegregate its education system, there have been many calls for magnet schools—places with special programs that attract students from different districts and give them an opportunity to learn something new, and to learn it together. That's happening in Bridgeport, in a program that takes advantage of the state's greatest natural resource.

There's something about a teacher taking a bunch of teenagers on a boat that has overtones of driver's ed. class.

"Aaah, okay, I'm not gonna hit that buoy," says the tenth grader, taking the wheel for the first time.

These are students from the Regional Aquaculture School, and they're learning about everything from water quality to marine critters. The students built the trap they're hauling onto the boat, a trap that's now filled with spider crabs.

The students are unlikely partners. They come from inner-city Bridgeport and six suburban towns, and they spend part of their school day together. For some, this is their first experience on Long Island Sound, though they may have grown up in a hous-

ing project less than a block from the harbor.

School Superintendent James Connelly: *"This school can really stand as a beacon for all of desegregation in Connecticut. Here we are in Bridgeport, Connecticut, next to the P. T. Barnum Housing Project, and we have seven school districts sending youngsters here."*

When they're not on the water, the students are in workshops learning skills like boat building and net tying. For some, that will lead to jobs in commercial fishing or boating.

For others, the school has opened up a whole new world.

Jasmyne Ortiz: *"I like dolphins and I want to be a marine biologist and this will give me a headstart in college. The simple fact is that all the whales are dying, and I want to do something to help them."*

Jasmyne will learn a lot of marine biology as the tanks she's tending become a hatchery for trout and shellfish. Shelves hold giant jars filled with bright green water. This is the stuff you don't want in your swimming pool. It's algae the students grow to feed the fish they're raising.

In the classroom, students learn about mapping oceans and plotting navigational courses. A teacher guides them. "Okay, now that's your latitude. Let's find your longitude."

Their laboratory is the Sound, so next semester the twenty-five-foot boat will be supplemented by three classrooms on board a fifty-six-foot boat that's being specially built.

The aquaculture program is broad. Some students use it to find careers, others to find themselves.

Teacher Tim Visel: *"When they come to us and get interested and excited and motivated about their schoolwork and going into a particular career, that's very nice to see."*

Diane asks a Bridgeport student what she has learned about the other kids.

Nidia Figueroa: *"Well, that they're different, that they're really trying for their goals, and they really want to do what they want to do."*

Chris Hopwood (from Fairfield): *"Everybody says all Bridgeport kids are tough, but I like meeting new people here. I've made some good friends."*

Students at the Aquaculture School are learning about more than the sea. They're learning about life, in an innovative program that's positively Connecticut.

SINCE OUR STORY:

The Aquaculture School has broadened its curriculum and collaborated with universities near and far. A study with the Shanghai Fisheries University led to the successful growth of two crops of bay scallops in the school's farm in the Sound. That study could lead to commercial scallop farming in the western end of the Sound.

The new fifty-six-foot vessel the Catherine Moore *has three main areas—a navigation classroom on the bridge, a science classroom in the main cabin, and a commercial fishing area. The curriculum now includes engine repair, marine electronics, boat design, and construction, marine restoration, commercial fishing, maritime history, and other marine sciences.*

Christmas at the People's Mansion

HARTFORD

For the past few years the public has been invited to visit the governor's residence during the Christmas season, and I have had the privilege of a personal tour with the First Lady. Christmas 1996 brought an especially lovely visit with First Lady Patty Rowland at the "People's Mansion."

As Christmas approaches, Patty Rowland is supervising the ongoing refurbishing of the residence. The entryway is now Wedgwood blue, painted in a style that makes it look paneled. Five varieties of poinsettias bank the grand staircase, donated by the florists and tree growers who deck the halls of the residence, free of charge.

Another new touch: The state seal, which reads *qui transtulit sustinet* ("that which is planted sustains"), has been worked into the wood floor in the front parlor.

Patty: *"We actually put a time capsule underneath, in case this house ever comes down in one hundred, two hundred, three hundred years from now, so they know what life was like here in 1996."*

The parlor's holiday tree is wrapped in mauve metallic French ribbon and hung with golden cherubs and blossoms of dried hydrangea. The formal dining room features

new silk damask wall covering. Dried amaranthus hangs like cranberry-colored icicles from the mantel.

In the living room, a tree is decorated with elaborate paper ornaments made by West Hartford artist Patty Kierys.

Patty: *"This is our tree of Connecticut historic attractions and famous people. And look who showed up on the tree this year."*

She points to an ornament made from my photograph.

Diane laughs: *"She looks familiar."*

The artist has dressed me in a pink crepe paper ballgown, and tucked my Sheltie puppy, Chester, under my arm.

We're in good company, side by side with the first family, Paul Newman, Mark Twain, Rebecca Lobo, Whoopi Goldberg, and others.

The sunroom is scented with a gingerbread village.

Patty: *"They represent historic buildings all over the state of Connecticut."*

Included are the Carousel at Lighthouse Point in New Haven, the Goodspeed Opera House in Haddam, and the Soldiers and Sailors Arch from Bushnell Park. The gingerbread is to be auctioned off for charity.

The sunroom tree is decorated with ornaments made or collected by the First Family's children. A singing Elvis, one of the governor's favorites, is making his first appearance.

In the library the First Lady's favorite tree is decorated with her own ornaments, lovingly collected over the years.

Diane offers a wrapped gift to Patty Rowland.

Diane: *"Maybe this will go with your ornaments. I thought you should have it."*

Patty takes out a wooden ornament shaped like the state, with the words "Christmas in Connecticut" inked across one side.

Patty: *"Christmas in Connecticut. Sounds like a movie. Oh that's beautiful. Let's hang it right in front."*

A tour of the governor's residence with First Lady Patty Rowland, a holiday tradition that's positively Connecticut. 🖎

MORE ABOUT THE GOVERNOR'S HOME:

Connecticut's governors did not have an official residence until 1943, when the state purchased the Georgian-style home that had been built by Dr. George C. F. Williams in 1908. The three-story house is brick and limestone, and although it had once been owned by one of Hartford's wealthiest families, by the time the state bought it for $39,000 (the amount owed in back taxes) it had long been vacant. Gov. Raymond Baldwin and his family moved in on September 14, 1945, after the house was refurbished. The 15,000-square-foot home has nineteen rooms, nine fireplaces, a greenhouse, and a reflecting pool set on several wooded acres. At $39,000 it may have been the real-estate find of the century.

Pinchbeck's Roses

GUILFORD

A rose by any other name may smell as sweet, but it may not be as fresh or as perfect as the roses named Pinchbeck's. Bill Pinchbeck's grandfather started the rose-growing business in the 1920s and the family business has been blooming in Guilford ever since.

Three million roses come out of Pinchbeck's quarter-mile-long greenhouse each year, even though Connecticut's climate is not the most conducive to growing flowers.

Bill Pinchbeck: *"The dark days of the winter in Connecticut make it difficult for us. We don't get the production that we'd like, and it's tough for us on Valentine's Day especially. We have our best holiday at the worst time of the year."*

The roses are under careful observation from the time the rice-grain-sized buds first appear.

Bill: *"It takes about three weeks to come to full bloom. So what we do is, we watch the bud size very carefully when we get close to a holiday because timing is crucial to our business, you know. You can't have the roses too late or too soon."*

When Valentine's Day approaches they can hardly come soon enough. The graders

FOLLOW-UP:

Tom Pinchbeck now runs the business along with his father, Bill. Tom and Bill resist jumping too quickly into trends in floral colors, since they keep each of their ninety thousand bushes in production for about six years. They are selling more purple roses, favored by Patty Rowland, wife of Connecticut Gov. John Rowland.

Patty started a mini-trend in purple roses during an interview with me shortly after she became first lady. I asked Patty, then a newlywed, if she considered her husband to be romantic. She paused for a moment, then blushed and revealed that he could send flowers more often. The governor's excuse? He couldn't find her favorite purple roses.

The next day a florist located them, a radio deejay delivered them, and the governor joked about it in several speeches that week. By the end of the week not only did Patty have a dozen long-stemmed beauties, but so did I, sent by Gov. and Mrs. Rowland. They're called "Lavande." I will always think of the purple variety as "Patty Rowland roses."

sort thousands per day, and they are picky, picky, picky.

Bill: *"They're looking for the proper stage of development of the bud, the right shape, that the leaves are clean and disease-free, stems are straight. If the rose is too open it's not good; if it's too tight they won't draw water."*

An infrared sensor separates the roses by the length of their stems. Twenty-six to thirty inches is top of the line.

Valentine's Day is the biggest single day of the year for America's florists. Some seventy million roses are sent by lovers to their sweethearts. About eighty percent of those are red. The favored red variety at Pinchbeck's is known as Forever Yours.

Changing fashions in home design have increased the popularity of pastel-colored roses, and Pinchbeck's grows eighteen varieties. But for Valentine's Day, people still want red roses. That's what Bill Pinchbeck sends his Valentine. Homegrown roses that are positively Connecticut.

Metamorphosis

SOUTHINGTON

*I*f Grandma handed down her mink stole to you, and you're not wearing it, Marion Virello may have the answer. Turn it into a teddy bear.

At her home in Southington, Marion has fashioned bears from almost every kind of old fur coat, from beaver, seal, Persian lamb, and mink. And she uses every bit of the coat. Fasteners become decorative buttons on bear bellies. Monogrammed linings become scarves. A shoulder pad makes a jaunty bow tie. An embroidered lining, a bear's foot pad.

Marion looks at it as recycling.

Marion: *"This is one way to not destroy what unfortunately was destroyed in the first place. It's not going to get thrown away, and it could be cherished for a family's lifetime."*

Although Marion's daughter Molly and her friend do find the bears cuddly, most of them are made for adult collectors.

Marion: *"They are heirlooms to be handed down from generation to generation. They're made from coats that were handed down from somebody's mother or grandmother, or great-grandmother."*

The sewing pattern took Marion four years to perfect. Even though she starts each bear with the same pattern, each one looks a little different. Some she dresses up.

Marion: *"This one reminds me of Grandma. My grandmother every Sunday would dress up in her fancy hat and shawl and go to church in her fancy earrings."*

Most of the bears stand sixteen inches tall, and cost between $75 and $95. But Marion has made bears as small as two and three-quarter inches tall. She made a teeny ballerina bear after seeing one like it at a teddy bear show. But she went one better. Figuring every ballerina needs music to dance to, Marion affixed this bear to a music box, and it pirouettes in time to the tune.

The tiniest bears are fashioned from velvet or fake fur. Their completely jointed bodies, with arms as thin as pipe cleaners, take ten painstaking hours to complete.

Marion: *"I have to use a pair of tweezers or a toothpick to turn their fur after I stitch it."*

But it's more than the craftsmanship that makes Marion's bears special.

Marion*: "It's more about the love that's put into them, and the memories that they bring back to the family."*

Memories that are positively Connecticut.

ONE MORE THING:

After this story aired, we were inundated with phone calls from people who wanted Marion's phone number so they could commission her to make teddy bears for them. When we aired the story again at the end of the year, more people called. I don't know if Marion will ever catch up, or ever forgive me.

Summer in the Country

There's a place in Connecticut where people are measured by what they can do, not by what they can't. It's a place where even kids in wheelchairs play softball, and sing around the campfire on starry nights.

A summer breeze, a glimmering pond, and the fish are biting. Sounds like a perfect day at summer camp. At this camp, you can roll your wheelchair right onto the dock for fishing.

Jonathan Slifka is spending his third summer at Easter Seals' Camp Hemlocks.

Jonathan: *"I've learned stuff that I'm not good at."*

Diane: *"Such as ?"*

Jonathan: *"Such as, I can't catch fish for anything!"*

But for most kids, this is a place to find out about all the things they *are* good at, in spite of their physical limitations.

The swimming pool is specially equipped so that even a quadriplegic can get into the soothing water.

Over the sounds of kids laughing and splashing, swimming instructor Lisa DeCarvaho explains.

Lisa: *"For most of them the pool is the place they are most comfortable. We try to work on a little bit of movement with their arms and legs,* whatever they can do. Some of them are actually very good swimmers despite their disabilities."

At Camp Hemlocks kids learn more than sports; they learn about life and about themselves.

Camper Rachel King: *"You get to make new friends here with different disabilities than you have. It doesn't make me feel so sorry for myself like sometimes I do when I'm alone in my room."*

Some campers don't have disabilities. They come for "buddy weekends," when they are paired with children with disabilities who have similar interests. Differences disappear pretty quickly.

At the arts and crafts center, children are working with clay and paints. Although she can't speak, Jennifer Johnston keeps the other campers laughing with her computerized voiceboard, which she has programmed to tell jokes.

In another building, a teenager with cerebral palsy is teaching other kids to use computers.

At a visitor's day barbecue, guests are pitching in, flipping burgers and pouring lemonade. Former camper Leo Germain is playing deejay. The kids are thinking about this evening, when some of them will camp out under the stars. They'll hike trails adapted for kids who depend on crutches. For children who have spent too much time in wheelchairs, and hospitals, and physical therapy rooms, Camp Hemlocks means the freedom they have never had.

John Quinn of the Easter Seal Society: *"We provide that opportunity for a child, not to spend the time in the bedroom or in the house in the middle of summer, but to be outdoors and enjoy it."*

It costs about $600 a week to send a kid to camp, but there are scholarships available. The people who donate to make perfect summer days at camp possible, make Easter Seals' Camp Hemlocks a place for kids that's positively Connecticut. 🔥

A FINAL WORD:

For years I've raised money for Camp Hemlocks, because I've seen what it can do for a child. Leo Germain says that at camp, his disability made him "one of the gang" and his every ability was challenged and encouraged. If only the rest of the world could be like Camp Hemlocks.

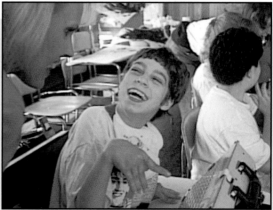

Stogies

*I*n the dry weather, sun-grown Connecticut tobacco hangs curing from the rafters of well-ventilated barns. In wet weather the barns are closed up, and charcoal fires burn in the sand floors to speed drying of the tobacco that will end up in the cigars made by F.D. Grave and Son.

In New Haven, manufacturer F. D. Grave and Son has used Connecticut broad-leaf tobacco for more than one hundred years in its Muniemaker-brand cigars. Fred Grave helps run the company started by his grandfather Frederick Grave in 1884.

Fred: *"He was a typically Germanic entrepreneur. He came to this country when he was eleven years old. He was one of eight or nine children in Germany. He came by himself."*

Today grandsons Fred and Dick and great granddaughter Dorothy run the business, turning out six and a half million cigars a year.

Fred: *"Connecticut sun-grown broad-leaf tobacco is a very natural hardy product. And as I say, it is full-bodied and has a lot of quality to it and substance to it."*

The first step in turning dried tobacco into cigars is moisturizing it in an antique bathtub. Once it's steamed, the "hand" of tobacco goes to the strippers, who remove the stems. Each operator strips about one hundred pounds of tobacco a day. Hand-rolling went out in the 1950s. Now the cigars are molded mostly by machine. Muniemakers are all-natural, all-Connecticut tobacco with no fillers and no additives. So are Grave's other brands: Judge's Cave and Bouquet Special.

The Graves like to say that their cigar-making hasn't really changed that much in their many years of business. They even have some machines that date back to the 1930s. But the cigar industry certainly has changed dramatically.

Dick: *"Until the time of the first World War, cigars were it as far as smoking was concerned. And I think the tops in the cigar industry was around 1914 when we sold maybe 15 million cigars that year. And since then it's been gradually downhill because the cigarette industry has taken over. It's a cigarette-smoking country, more than a cigar-smoking country."*

In the early 1900s New Haven boasted some twenty cigar factories. Now F. D. Grave is one of only two cigar companies left in all of New England.

Fred: *"I think once you get in it, it's kind of infectious . . . I think your life develops around accepting this kind of responsibility and risk. It's a very full life and a very rewarding life, though it doesn't have the security perhaps of working for a larger corporation."*

It's a life that has attracted a fourth generation in the Grave family. Dorothy works side by side with her uncle and her father.

Dorothy: *"Our product will stay the same. We have a product and it is a good product and we will never change it."*

Ensuring that for some time to come, cigar-making will remain positively Connecticut. ❧

SINCE OUR STORY:

So much for predictions! In 1985, facing a shrinking pool of semiskilled workers, F. D. Grave moved its production to Pennsylvania. Muniemakers and Judge's Cave cigars are still made with all-Connecticut tobacco, though, and company headquarters is still on State Street in New Haven. The company has started an imported line sold under the F. D. Grave brand name. They ship Connecticut tobacco to Honduras, where it is hand-rolled. Those premium cigars sell for about $3.50 to $4.50, while the Muniemaker and Judge's Cave retail for about a dollar each.

Callaway Corvettes

OLD LYME

Every good reporter has a little Walter Mitty in him or her. My biggest joy as a reporter is getting the opportunity to do things other people only dream about. What red-blooded American wouldn't want to drive a super-charged Corvette? I not only had the chance to drive one, but I did it with the man who designed it.

A sleek red Corvette is as all-American as Old Glory. Reeves Callaway designed the custom body for the Chevrolet, but his heart is really under the hood.

Reeves: *"The engine is the part of the car that lives. The engine is where the noise happens. It's what makes the music. Secondarily it's also sort of what propels you around."*

Propels? This ultra-souped-up Vette *explodes* in a breathtaking burst of speed. Callaway Corvettes are guaranteed to do 195 miles an hour, powered by Callaway's specially designed turbocharging system.

Reeves: *"When you push the starter button on a new engine design and it comes to life for the first time, that thing has a life of its own and you just created it."*

Like the one he's creating for an Aston Martin racing car.

Old Lyme may seem like an unusual place

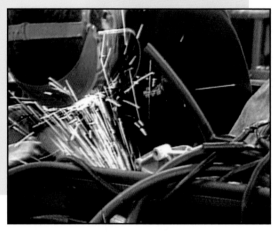

for a laboratory that invents racing car engines. When you pull up outside Callaway's and see the French military helicopter Reeves flies in his spare time, you know this is no ordinary factory.

And Reeves Callaway is no ordinary hot-rodder. He was an art major in college, which may be why he cares so much not only about how each part in his engine performs, but also about how it looks.

Reeves has forged an unusual relationship with auto giant General Motors. A conversion to a Callaway Corvette is an option you can order from your Chevrolet dealer. The car is built at the GM plant in Kentucky, then shipped to Callaway in Old Lyme, where everything from the radiator up front to the fuel pumps in the rear are replaced with parts that are computer-designed and crafted by men with gasoline running through their veins. It's a mass-production car with a boutique finish.

The Callaway Corvette has been named the fastest street car in the world. And Callaway's racing version, the Sledgehammer, was clocked at 254 miles an hour.

Reeves: *"When we said that we will go 250 miles an hour in a road-based vehicle that you can drive from here to Ohio and back again, there were a lot of snickers."*

Nobody's laughing now at the Callaway Corvettes that are positively Connecticut.

Hair of the Dog

SOUTHPORT

Pet owners sometimes greet the warmth of spring with mixed emotions. It's the time of year when shedding becomes a big problem around the house. But there's a Southport woman who has figured out how to put that annoying mess to good use.

The thick, white fur coat that kept Nikita warm through winter is piling up around the house now. But Kendall Crolius says "stop vacuuming and start knitting." The Southport ad executive has been known to make mittens from a malamute, or a beret from a beagle.

Kendall: *"The initial reaction is usually one of absolute shock or horror. They just think it's revolting or cruel to animals or something like that. I think people sense that I'm out there shearing dogs. We definitely don't do that. We don't recommend that. You just collect the fuzz by brushing your dog the way you ordinarily would, so the dogs love it."*

She came up with the idea while learning to spin yarn from sheep's wool.

Kendall: *"Spinning is this incredible process and, you know, we've been doing it for thousands of years. Dog hair is just slightly trickier than wool to spin because the fibers are a little slipperier but it's very much like spinning*

angora or cashmere, and the yarn you end up with is much like cashmere or angora. Very beautiful with a sort of soft fuzzy halo."

She tells you how to "put on the dog" in her book, *Knitting with Dog Hair.*

Kendall: *"It was just published in England last fall and it's absolutely selling like hot cakes over there. The British are just nuts for their dogs and very much into handicrafts so it's perfect for over there."*

She admits even dog lovers have some concerns about getting into the fashion doghouse.

Kendall: *"That's the other big question: Do you smell like a wet dog when it rains? And the answer is absolutely not. I mean, I don't know if you've ever spent any time around wet sheep but it's really much less appealing than a wet dog, and yet we don't worry about our sweaters smelling like a wet sheep. Just as with wool you wash the dog yarn or dog hair before you spin it."*

A few folks have even greater worries.

Kendall: *"People have asked me, 'If you're driving down the street in your dog hair sweater, will you have the urge to stick your head out the window?' Absolutely not! There's nothing about this that makes you behave like a dog."*

For some people, that dog hair scarf can be a final memento of their pet.

Kendall: *"I have gotten several very poignant letters from people who said, 'Oh, I'm so glad I got your book. I made these mittens and then little Fluffy passed away but I still have the mittens.'"*

So the next time you're reaching for the lint brush, think about recycling Rover's hair into something you can wear. Kendall swears her dog steps a little prouder when they go walking and Kendall is wearing a matching sweater.

Kendall Crolius is knitting with dog hair, making fetching designs that are positively Connecticut. 🐾

THE REST OF THE STORY:

Ultra-tony Southport is a place you generally expect to find people clad in cashmere or mink, not garments made from dog hair. Kendall Crolius has one of the more unusual hobbies in her neighborhood. Folks there know all about it, since in the warm weather Kendall sets up her spinning wheel on the front porch.

Kendall's book is selling well, which comes as a surprise to a lot of the people in publishing. Knitting with Dog Hair *has the distinction of being the work that was rejected by more publishers than any other book that eventually went on to be published. It was featured in an article in the* Wall Street Journal *about the trials of getting a book into print. People who saw the article started asking for the book, and St. Martin's Griffin Press had to rush to meet the demand.*

What kind of dog hair is best? While Kendall maintains that the hair of any breed is spinnable—except the Mexican hairless—it's clear a golden retriever has it all over a Great Dane.

A Living Past

Avon / © Jack McConnell

Legacy of a Slave Ship

NEW HAVEN

The Amistad story is now known world-wide, thanks to the Steven Spielberg film released in 1997. But for years several groups in Connecticut have been dedicated to telling that story. One of them is the Connecticut Afro-American Historical Society, based in New Haven.

A small, tired-looking building on Orchard Street in New Haven houses a proud heritage. It is the home of the Connecticut Afro-American Historical Society. The president is George Bellinger, who points out a passage from a historical account that indicates Africans were among the earliest settlers of the colony.

George: *"Lucretia was a slave to New Haven's first governor in 1638, Governor Eaton, which indicates that we've been here since 1638 and have participated in this society."*

The library contains three thousand volumes written by or about African Americans. Many of the books are out of print and not available anywhere else. One tiny book details the New Haven census of 1840.

Diane: *"So what does the census tell us then about the people who were living here at that time?"*

George: *"Well actually it appears to say*

that in 1840 that there was some semblance of integration because they included the blacks who were here."

The collection traces the important contributions of African Americans outside Connecticut, too. An engraving depicts senators and congressmen elected during the Reconstruction Era following the Civil War. A series of busts commemorates people like Matthew Henson, who explored the North Pole with Perry, and Lewis Lattimer, who helped Edison in his work with electricity. And there's Dr. Charles Drew, who discovered blood plasma. He died because he needed a blood transfusion following a car accident and a Southern hospital refused to treat him. He was black, and the hospital was for whites only.

Photographs show African Americans gathered for family portraits. There are church congregations and military platoons. There are photos commemorating shops and hotels owned by blacks and the first black Boy Scout troop in the United States. It was organized in New Haven in 1914.

FOR MORE ON THE AMISTAD STORY:

The sites where events in the Amistad story took place are now among the eighty locations in dozens o f communities that make up the Connecticut Freedom Trail. According to its organizers, these sites tell the "story of the struggle for freedom, justice, and equality in Connecticut from 1600 to 1947." A series of audiotapes guides you on four separate tours in your car. The "North Central Connecticut Tour" begins at the Old State House in Hartford, where the Amistad trial took place in the Senate chambers. It also includes the house where Harriet Beecher Stowe wrote Uncle Tom's Cabin, *the home where black singer and actor Paul Robeson lived, and several homes that were stops on the underground railroad. For information about how to purchase copies of the auto-tour tapes and for more information about the Amistad story contact:*

The Amistad Committee
P.O. Box 2936 Westville Station
New Haven, CT 06515
(203) 387–0370

AMISTAD America

George reads aloud from a page in a 1926 New Haven newspaper.

George: *"It says, 'News of interest for our colored readers.' All the news about black folks was on one page in the paper."*

The Society is dedicated in part to getting out the story of the slave ship *La Amistad,* which carried men and women who were captured in Africa.

George: *"The Amistad captives were being transferred in Cuba and took over the ship and ordered the navigator to sail them home. In the daytime he would slowly head toward Africa, but at nighttime he would head back toward America. The zigzag course took them off Long Island and the Coast Guard picked them up and they brought them to New Haven."*

It would take several years to resolve, but eventually the Amistad case would become the first civil rights matter to go all the way to the U.S. Supreme Court, where the Africans finally won their freedom.

The leader of those captives, Cinque, has become the symbol of the Connecticut Afro-American Historical Society, which honors him with a monument outside New Haven City Hall. It is part of the legacy of the Society, a legacy that is positively Connecticut. 🎐

SINCE OUR STORY:

The Afro-American Historical Society's mission to teach Connecticut and America about the Amistad case went well beyond the erection of the monument in front of New Haven City Hall. George Bellinger now heads Amistad America Inc., which is devoted to the re-creation of the free-dom schooner Amistad. *Connecticut is funding the construction with a $2.5 million bond issue. The keel on the 85-foot, hand-hewn vessel was laid at Mystic Seaport in March 1998 while two thousand people looked on. Construction of the "freedom schooner" is due to be completed by the year 2000, and the* Amistad *will then set sail to domestic and international ports as a floating museum and classroom. During construction the vessel is on display at Mystic Seaport. To follow its progress check the Amistad America Web site at http://www.amistadamerica.org.*

The sculptor of the Amistad monument outside New Haven City Hall is Ed Hamilton of Louisville, Kentucky, who is known for his portrayals of African American heroes.

A more recent work by Hamilton is called Spirit of Freedom, the 12-foot bronze centerpiece of the African American Civil War Memorial in Washington, D.C. The Washington monument was unveiled on July 19, 1998, the 135th anniversary of the assault on Fort Wagner, South Carolina, by the 54th Massachusetts, the black regiment memorialized in the 1990 film Glory. The sculpture depicts three black soldiers and one black sailor, signifying the 208,000 black troops who fought in the Civil War, including the all-black 29th Connecticut Volunteer Infantry. Eventually the monument will include walls inscribed with the names of all the black troops and their white commanding officers.

The Grand Army

VERNON

Before the American Legion, there was the Grand Army of the Republic, a powerful organization of hundreds of thousands of Civil War veterans who fought on the Union side. A GAR group in Vernon is dedicated to preserving the history of the veterans' service to this country.

On the second Thursday of every month for more than a hundred years, an elegant chamber in the Vernon Town Hall has been the meeting place for Union veterans of the Civil War—and then their sons, their grandsons, and their great grandsons. The chamber looks much the same as it did when the town hall was constructed, as a monument to the Grand Army of the Republic.

Richard Wassener, a member of the Alden Skinner Camp of the GAR, describes the uniform he is wearing.

Richard: *"This would probably be around 1885, when some of the GAR camps adopted the Indian War jacket."*

Like Wassener, many of today's GAR members are direct descendants of Union veterans. Camp commander Guy Minor has followed in the footsteps of his great-great-uncle.

Guy: *"This is a photo of Samuel Kimball Ellis. (He points to an old photo framed on the wall.) This is him as commander in 1898 of the GAR."*

Ross Dent wears a button that nine of his great-great-uncles might have worn.

Ross: *"They could wear that on all their civilian clothes, so everybody in the public knew that they were a member of the Grand Army of the Republic. It's important to remember that back in those days, the men of the Grand Army of the Republic were revered, for saving the Union."*

Three years ago Dent and other members began converting the meeting room into the New England Civil War Museum

Ross: *"We feel that this came to us and we know that we must hand it to the next generation."*

Without any grants or corporate contributions, the group has acquired some significant collections. Members raised $9,000 to buy memorabilia of Col. Thomas Burpee, who was shot in Cold Harbor in 1864, died on June 11 of that year, and is buried in Vernon.

The Burpee collection includes his hand-painted escutcheon, outlining his wartime career. And it includes the bullet that killed him. There's also a condolence letter from Governor Buckingham to Burpee's widow, Adeline.

Dent reads the governor's words.

Ross: *"He gave his life to his country, leaving this testimony that he was a pure patriot, fearless soldier, and a sincere Christian."*

Other local veterans are remembered here, too, including three brothers who fought and came home.

The museum's library preserves some very important records—a priceless resource for people trying to trace their lineage and find out if a relative was indeed a veteran of the Civil War. Camp members hope that as people discover the museum, precious relics will come out of basements and attics and become part of this tribute to local heroes of the Civil War, a tribute that's positively Connecticut.

UPDATE:

The museum's most significant artifacts are still those of Colonel Burpee, a mill worker from the Rockville section of Vernon, who served in the 21st Connecticut Volunteer Infantry. The artifacts had been part of the private collection of Burpee's great-niece. When her estate went on the auction block, members of the Alden Skinner Camp were determined to buy the Burpee memorabilia. Starting on a Monday, which happened to be Memorial Day, they put out an appeal to the public. By Saturday's auction they had raised $2,300, mostly in contributions of a few dollars apiece from local people. Ross Dent and his friends were able to buy some of the primary objects, and they later raised more money to buy additional pieces, including Burpee's sash and his pay records. Their effort has been noted by the head of the Gettysburg Preservation Society as the first time a town has banded together to buy back the historic items of a fallen son.

Sleigh Bells Ring

HADDAM

People always say winters in Connecticut aren't like they used to be. Seems everyone remembers winters that were colder, and deep in snow. But John and Kate Allegra don't reminisce much about the past, because they live it every day, in the present. They've revived an era when a snowstorm didn't shut down interstate highways, because there weren't any. In their world a snowstorm means an opportunity to hitch up a matched pair of bays, bundle up in bearskin, and set off on a trail through the woods.

It's a scene right out of a Currier and Ives print. A coachman cloaked in bearskin, a Victorian lady in a bonnet, and a horse-drawn sleigh. John and Kate Allegra operate their fantasy farm in Haddam, colored with the character of another era.

Four-year-old Tucker Norman and his mom have come to Allegra Farm for a ride.
Diane: *"What do you think of this?"*
Tucker: *"Ooooh, I like the big horses."*

John restores his fleet of carriages himself. Kate collects the vintage costumes that help set the mood.

John: *"This is as close as you'll ever get to the real thing, because it is the real thing."*

And for passengers all wrapped up under

buffalo lap robes, it feels like the real thing. With snow flying under the blades of the sleigh, it's enough to make you feel like singing, and pretty soon we are, breaking into a hearty chorus of "Jingle Bells."

"Dashing through the snow, in a one-horse open sleigh."

The sleigh winds its way through the fields and woods of the Allegras' twelve acres and the thirty acres they lease as pasture. As twilight draws near, there's romance in the air.

John: *"We've actually had people propose in sleighs in the middle of a blizzard. I'm always hoping she'll say yes, and there haven't been any yet that have gone astray."*

Maybe that's because this sleigh brought John and Kate together. They each ran carriage companies, and met at an auction in Pennsylvania.

Kate (laughing): *"We ended up bidding on the same sleigh and he got it, but he had to pay a lot more!"*

John: *"She got one and I got one, and now we have them both."*

The Allegras share a passion for the past that led them to build a 12,000-square-foot barn, gleaming now with fresh white paint and decked in pine roping.

John: *"The barn is post-and-beam that we built from the hemlock that is native to the area."*

They've filled the barn with carriages and sleighs, even two horse-drawn hearses. Soon visitors will be able to watch as John restores carriages and harnesses.

The Allegras run sleigh rides every day as long as the snow holds up. But they hold events for all seasons. In the warm weather you can join them for an authentic chuck-wagon supper, complete with costumed ranch hands and entertainment around the campfire.

John: *"We meet a lot of special people. We make dreams come true, and that's what it's all about."*

Yes, that's what it's all about at Allegra Farm—a sleigh ride into the past that's positively Connecticut. 🖋

A CLOSER LOOK:

I'd met John Allegra before, when his collection of sleighs and carriages was smaller. Most of his business at the time was taking brides to their weddings in open carriages and providing authentic transportation for costumed interpreters at Mystic Seaport. I'd ridden in one of his carriages and watched him repair a huge wooden wheel in his barn—activities I thought only went on in living museums like the Seaport or Sturbridge Village, not in a real person's backyard.

Since this story, John and Kate have filed for non-profit status and are seeking grants to help them develop Allegra Farm as a working museum. And the Allegras have "Gone Hollywood." You'll see John and his carriages and horses in the Steven Spielberg epic Amistad, *shot partly on location at Mystic Seaport.*

The Lady of the House

MERIDEN

When Bernice Shelberg dons her Colonial-era costume to answer the door at the Solomon Goffe house, she really seems like the lady of the house. And in a way she is. This is the oldest house in Meriden, built in 1711. But it wouldn't be standing today, if not for Bernice.

The story of Bernice and the Goffe House goes back to 1976, the year of the U.S. bicentennial.

Bernice: *"The house was just about to be torn down, as it was in very bad shape. And I thought, well we can't do that. It's the oldest house in our city and it has got to be restored."*

She persuaded Napier, the jewelry company, to donate the house to the city. Then Bernice began a campaign to raise $200,000 to restore it. She enlisted her husband, John, to start the repairs.

Bernice: *"I think a lot of people thought I'd never do it, and I'm sure that many times during the years I wondered myself if I was going to be able to do it!"*

Now most of the house is refurbished and furnished with reproductions of the furniture that belonged to Solomon Goffe.

Bernice: *"He was a young man of twenty-eight years old. He was married, had a wife,*

Elizabeth, and a small girl child. He had inherited a hundred acres here from his father, who was Erin Goffe, who had a store in Wethersfield."

Bernice shows us a bed chamber furnished as it might have been when the Goffes called this home.

Bernice: *"Our bed is a pencil-post bed, with a canopy. These curtains close for warmth in the wintertime. You would close yourself completely in the bed and be warm, as all that would heat this room would be our small little fireplace."*

The holidays are an especially good time to visit. The house is all decked out for Christmas, and candlelight tours are given. Volunteers are busy for weeks making period decorations for the tree. There are cornucopias stuffed with treats, and small wreaths made from dried slices of fruit. Karen Keene leads a class in Colonial decorating.

Karen: *"We have some dried apples that we've strung up on rings, and we tie them with ribbons. These will be used to hang either on the Christmas tree or in the windows."*

Throughout the year, and especially at Christmas time, Bernice Shelberg shares her gift to Meriden with all of us, a gift that is positively Connecticut. 🖋

SINCE OUR STORY:

The second story is now open, featuring a children's room and spinning room. The basement is finished, too, as a so-called summer kitchen. Eighteenth-century suppers and candlelight tours have helped pay for these renovations. Bernice has made restoration and preservation of the Goffe House something of a family affair. Her husband worked on the initial repairs, and now her son, a building contractor, is donating his services. She proudly notes that this has all been accomplished "without taxpayer dollars."

The Friends of the Solomon Goffe House hold "living history" programs the first Sunday of every month. They involve classes in anything from open-hearth cooking to felting, the technique early Americans used to turn sheep's wool into the fabric for making hats.

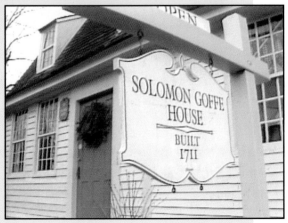

Walking Weekend

MANSFIELD

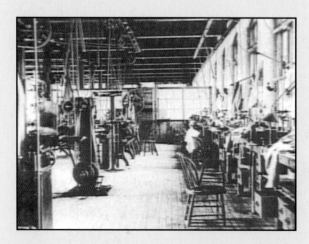

The most beautiful time of year in Connecticut may be when the fall foliage makes its showy appearance. If a nice walk in the crisp fall air sounds appealing, you may want to visit Connecticut's Quiet Corner over Columbus Day weekend.

They call it the Quiet Corner of Connecticut, and there is a serenity to its beauty. In 1994 the Quinebaug and Shetucket Rivers Valley was designated a National Heritage Corridor, encompassing twenty-five towns from Woodstock and Thompson to the north, south to Voluntown and Norwich, and west to Coventry. All over the region on Columbus Day weekend, local volunteers lead guided walking tours.

Kay Holt is the innkeeper at Fitch House and one of several guides for a walk dubbed "Mansfield Hollow, Past and Present." We met at the Mansfield Hollow Dam, which straddles lovely Lake Naubestuck. The dam was built to stop severe flooding downstream in Norwich and New London, but it was controversial here because its construction claimed part of the village. Two hundred families lost property, and some thirty homes were lost or moved.

Kay: *"The whole village is like stuck in amber.*

The dam stopped the road, and since then this village has stood still in time."

In the shadow of the dam, on the banks of the Natchaug River, stands the old Kirby Mill that once brought prosperity to Mansfield.

Althea Stadler's grandfather worked in the mill.

Althea: *"In the 1800s the silk industry became very very important to Mansfield. They raised silkworms, they spun silk, and by 1830 they were spinning silk right here in Mansfield Hollow."*

The mill later went on to make thread, then optical goods. Some of the antique eyeglasses were still there when the University of Connecticut moved into the building a few years ago.

A retired professor who lives in the hollow, David Hall, showed us the historic homes.

David: *"This house is Greek Revival in style and is influenced by the structure of Greek temples."*

Hall's own house is a legacy of the industry that once thrived here. He lives in the house Oliver Bingham built in 1790, when Bingham owned the mill.

David: *"The homes in the hollow also reflect the wealth and the health of the industry of the area."*

The boom-and-bust economy of the town is examined at the Mansfield Historical Society museum, in an exhibit included as part of the walking tour.

"Mansfield Hollow, Past and Present" is one of fifty-four walks offered in the "quiet corner" region over the three-day weekend. There are walks of every length and for every taste, whether you love history or art or wine or nature. "Hands Across the Border" takes you hiking along the Pachaug Trail that goes into Rhode Island.

If you care to stay over and make a weekend of it, the area boasts numerous bed-and-breakfast accommodations. There's the elegant Fitch House in Mansfield, and two of my favorites, Chickadee Cottage in Pomfret and Friendship Valley in Brooklyn.

The "walking weekend" in Connecticut's quiet corner, in twenty-five towns and villages, is an annual event that's positively Connecticut.

MORE ABOUT THE STORY:

One intriguing walk, titled "Stones and Bones," involves vampire hunting in Jewett City. We met historian Mary Deveau at the cemetery, where she told us the tale of Henry and Lucy Ray, whose son Lemuel died of tuberculosis in 1845. Consumption, as the wasting disease was then known, claimed Henry next, then another son, Elisha. By 1854, when the eldest son, Henry Nelson Ray, started coughing, the remaining Rays decided to fight back. They believed that Lemuel and Elisha were not truly dead but were vampires who fed on the living, causing them to waste away and die. In a late-night ritual, they dug up their remains and burned them to stop them from preying upon the family.

Another walk takes visitors to the new UConn Depot campus. One cottage has a most joyful population, the puppets of the Ballard Institute. Frank Ballard taught puppetry at UConn for thirty years, where the puppets appeared in operas, musicals, and plays. Parkinson's disease forced Frank to retire, but he says, "When God shuts one door, He opens a window." That window is the museum that brings the puppets to a new audience.

Survivor

STAFFORD SPRINGS

When sheep grazing in a meadow was a common sight in Connecticut, so was the sight of woolen mills. At one time there were thirteen mills in Stafford Springs alone.

Warren Mill, built in 1883, is renowned for its luxury fabrics: camel hair and cashmere. It is one of the last survivors of the woolen mills in Stafford Springs.

Linda Lastoff, mill store supervisor: *"Our camel hair comes from a Bactrian camel, which is a two-humped camel, and it's collected by people called 'trailers' who follow the herds around and pick it up as it molts off in the spring. The cashmere comes from a goat from China, and that's combed or collected off bushes that the animal walks by."*

That fleece is declumped, dyed, and blown through air ducts to different departments in the mill, where is it spun and spooled onto bobbins for weaving. To create cloth, a loom needs warp, the threads that make up its length, and woof, the threads that fill in. The pattern is set in a harness made up of hundreds of flat needles.

After the fabric comes off the loom, menders repair the tiniest flaws. Rose Bradnan, mending supervisor, points out

that there could be a pick that's missing—that's a thread out of the cloth.

Rose: *"A mender will recognize it and she will replace it, by sewing it back in, the same thread that was left out."*

Raymond Fontaine is running the loom.

Raymond: *"This is almost twice as fast as the old loom. We're putting out almost two times the picks we used to put out in the old-type loom. Being at it twenty-eight years, I sort of grew up with the job."*

In the finishing department the material is washed and dried, and the nap is raised with wire brushes, then sheared to even it out.

One of the most fascinating machines is the gig, used to put a sheen on certain kinds of material, like billiard cloth. To get that sheen the gig brushes the fabric with dried weeds, called teazels, that look like thistles. They're harvested in France.

Warren Mill is the nation's biggest supplier of camel hair and one of only two makers of cashmere.

A young woman tells us the fabrics are *"very warm and very lightweight and very soft, so when you feel it on yourself, it's a wonderful feeling."*

In many ways the old mill hasn't changed much in more than a century. Ten percent of its power is still generated by a waterwheel.

Once you've finished a tour, you can drop by the factory store and try on a luxurious blazer, sewn from the camel hair fabric made next door. Even if the camel is from Asia, the garment is positively Connecticut.

UPDATE:

Loro Piana, an Italian company, bought the plant in 1988 and has brought in its own technology from Italy. The Warren Mill now uses high-tech equipment to turn out wool and worsted wool in addition to cashmere and camel hair. One of its threads is so fine that if you unwound a one-pound skein of yarn, it would stretch for thirty miles. Tours are by appointment only, for groups of seven or more. The mill store has been closed, but you can buy items made from the fabrics at the Loro Piana store in New York City.

Historic Spirits

At Halloween the ghosts come out at one of my favorite historic houses in Connecticut, but if you listen carefully, you may hear their spirits whispering whenever you visit.

The front door creaks open and reveals a ghoulish face. There is a cackle of eerie laughter and an invitation:

"Welcome. Come in. My name is the Deacon John Grave."

Lots of houses claim to be haunted at Halloween, but this house, the Deacon John Grave House—well, there are people who say this house is haunted all year-round. And why not? The same family lived here for three hundred years, so where else would their spirits linger?

Fran Donnelly is the Madison town historian. Dressed in Colonial garb, she takes us through the home.

The Deacon John Grave II raised his ten children in this house. The entire family slept in one room, dormitory style. His son John III became the town justice of the peace and used the downstairs room as a courthouse.

You may still hear him presiding in one of the dramatic reenactments presented at the house. Fred, an angry farmer, is petitioning the court.

Fred: *"I'm tired of these sheep, they are in my garden again."*

John III: *"Broken fence again? Second time?"*

Fred: *"Second time. I cannot tolerate this any longer. They've destroyed my entire crop of carrots, absolutely gone."*

John: *"I think I must prepare a writ against your neighbor."*

Fred: *"It is time, sir."*

John: *"I must take some evidence from you, but I cannot do it today. I am too busy."*

Much of what we know about the family comes from reading a ledger, an account of their purchases and debts. It shows that the family sheltered British soldiers. It's believed that a daughter, Ann, fell in love with one of them but that he went away and never returned to marry her.

Some say she still waits.

Ann sits at the spinning wheel, sobbing.

Ann: *"He's not coming back, Mother, he's not coming back."*

Mother: *"You don't know, he may very well."*

Ann: *"I think he's been killed in the war."*

Mother: *"You've got to believe, you've got to hope."*

Ann: *"I think he is dead, else he would have come for me. I know he would have come back to me."*

The home on Madison's green was built in 1685. By 1702 the Post Road went by here, making the Grave home a convenient stopover on the route from New York to Boston. John III's son Elias opened a tavern and operated an inn in the house. It may have been in this tavern that Elias told his wife he'd be leaving to fight in the Revolution.

The Graves kept the home in the family until the early 1980s. When it was threatened with demolition, a group of Madison residents set up a foundation to buy and save the house and its heritage. They rescued one of the oldest shoreline homes that is positively Connecticut. 🪶

MORE ABOUT THIS STORY:

The Haunted House is an annual Halloween event at the Grave home, attracting lines of people who wait as long as two hours for a peek.

Sometime after doing our story, we returned to the Deacon John Grave House for another piece, this time about an exhibit from the Smithsonian that was displayed there. "After the Revolution" told the story of the emerging American nation from the end of the Revolution until the ratification of the Constitution. As Grave House supporter Diantha Allenby points out, the house was the perfect setting to tell the story: "The issues that shaped the nation were discussed within these walls. By 1783 this house was already in its third generation of ownership."

The Covered Bridge

EAST HAMPTON

At one time nearly forty covered bridges spanned the streams and rivers of Connecticut. Now there are barely a handful.

The Comstock Bridge has linked Colchester and East Hampton at the Salmon River since 1791. By the time the bridge was renovated by the Civilian Conservation Corps in the 1930s, it had been through its share of troubles. The bridge washed away at least twice. Then there was the time a beer truck fell through the floor of the bridge and into the river. Fortunately the neighbors were able to save the beer. Today, the bridge is open to foot traffic only.

Protecting the timbers and preventing the floors from collapsing in these wooden structures is said to be the reason for enclosing the bridges, though not everyone agrees. Andy Howard has traveled the world studying covered bridges and has written a guide to the ones still standing in Connecticut. He says enclosing the bridges may have made it easier to persuade horses and livestock to cross the river.

Andy: *"One speculation is that it made horses think they were heading into the barn, and that made them feel more comfortable."*

*The West Cornwall covered
bridge links the towns of
Cornwall and Sharon, which
are divided by the Housatonic
River. There has been a bridge
at the site since as early as
1762, according to Michael
Gannett of the Cornwall
Historical Society. The bridge
was threatened over the
years by ice jams on the river,
one of which was broken up
by dynamite. Another time a
fire on a hay truck flared up
as it went through the bridge.
In 1945 a twenty-ton oil truck
crashed through the floor
and into the river. The state
repaired and reinforced the
bridge and later won an
award for its preservation.
Occasionally over the years,
the bridge has been shut
down for an afternoon or
evening and converted into
the scene of a community
square dance. The tradition
was revived recently and a
covered bridge dance is held
Memorial Day weekend as a
fund raiser for the Cornwall
Volunteer Fire Department.*

He points out the carpentry details that have stood the test of time.

Andy: *"This is a tree nail, also known as a trunnell. And these wooden
pegs helped hold the bridge together. That's before steel bands were used for
preservation."*

If you've ever stopped at a covered bridge on an autumn day, you've
probably been caught in its spell.

Andy: *"One of the side effects of the covered bridges was that a shy suit-
or could pull inside with his sweetheart and steal a kiss in the shadows."*

Metro and Mary Maichak took time from their afternoon stroll to reminisce.

Metro: *"As a youngster we would dive off them into the creeks on hot
summer days and we enjoyed them very much."*

Diane: *"I've heard they are called kissing bridges."*

Mary: *"Oh, we wouldn't know. [She smiles.] And if we did, we wouldn't
tell."*

You can experience the romance of covered bridges in East Hampton,
West Cornwall, and Kent. Covered bridges, relics that are positively
Connecticut. ♪

Memories of War

DANBURY

I n Danbury there's a museum where every day is Veteran's Day.

Like most Americans his age, John Valluzzo grew up hearing all about World War II and the sacrifice and service of its veterans. But when John later completed his own period of Army service, he thought he was done with the military for good.

John: *"A friend of mine said, 'John, my uncle was a tank destroyer in World War II and no one is preserving their history.' And I said, 'So, what does that mean?'"*

What it meant was a decade of dedication that led John Valluzzo and a few of his friends to open the Military Museum of Southern New England. Director Philip Cocchiola showed me the military vehicle that started it all.

Philip: *"This is the M-18 tank destroyer. It was built by Buick in 1943 and '44. There are only three of these in the country. We have one that runs."*

John found the M-18 in Yugoslavia in 1987.

John: *"They wanted a trade, but since we are not in the arms business, I couldn't. So I went to Belgrade and convinced them to donate it to us."*

The museum's collection now numbers

more than fifty vehicles, including a tank that dates to World War I and tanks that saw service in World War II, Vietnam, Korea, even the Gulf War. There are ground-warfare vehicles from the other side, too, like a rare Soviet armored car.

Philip: *"This particular one was captured in Korea during the Korean War."*

For nine years the site in Danbury looked like a used tank lot. There was a trailer, surrounded by the expanding collection of vehicles. But a year ago the exhibit hall opened, built entirely with private money. Inside are life-size dioramas, contrasting with re-creations of battle scenes so tiny that each fighting man is barely the size of a grain of rice.

And there's personal memorabilia donated by veterans and their families. Some of that is displayed in an exhibit called "Memories of You," a sentimental collection of gifts that service people sent home to their sweethearts, including souvenir pillows, poems, and snapshots.

One third of the visitors are schoolkids, and John Valluzzo hopes they leave with one particular idea.

John: *"We are a free country today because of the sacrifices that our fathers and forefathers have made. We are the greatest country on the face of this earth, and we will continue to be so, as long as we keep in mind what democracy is and what it takes to preserve it."*

A Veterans' Day message that's positively Connecticut.

FOLLOW-UP:

The museum continues to expand, with volunteers now working on the second floor, which will house a library of more than three thousand volumes on military history as well as photo albums and personal recollections of Connecticut veterans. The vehicle collection is growing, too, with acquisition of a Soviet-made armored fighting machine and an anti-aircraft gun. Both were captured from the Iraqis by the First Marine Division in Kuwait during the Gulf War.

The museum is trying to acquire an adjacent tract of land for a vehicle park, complete with a driving trail. For now they offer rides in some of the tanks and other vehicles on special "open-turret days" at nearby Tarrywile Park.

White Squall

Tod Johnstone is an artist who crafts meticulous boat models at his Anguilla Gallery in Stonington. But for many years, he has had to carry the burden of a terrible memory: the 1961 sinking of the schooner Albatross.

Tod Johnstone sums up his experience on the *Albatross* this way.

Tod: *"As the ancient mariner says, 'The albatross hung about my neck,' and it almost hung my neck."*

Tod was seventeen years old when he set sail on the *Albatross,* a floating classroom, in hopes of finding his way in life.

Tod: *"I'd been to probably half the boarding schools in New England and had transcripts as thick as the New York yellow pages. I thought 'D' meant delightful—and 'A' meant awful, so I never had any of those."*

After months of cruising the tropics, the *Albatross* headed home to Mystic. In the Gulf of Mexico the schooner encountered a sudden violent storm. Tod was at the wheel.

Tod: *"I saw a cloud of mist as this white squall thing was headed our way. I tried to steer into it to address it. I heard the command to steer away, but I thought that was wrong, so I kept trying to head into it."*

Meteorologists call it a microburst—a heavy, dense, cold column of air that drops straight down, hitting the water, raising winds of 150 miles per hour. But sailors call it a white squall.

The ship turned on its side. Tod swam to the charthouse, where he knew people were trapped, but he couldn't save them.

In ninety seconds the boat was gone. Six people perished. The survivors, mostly teenage boys, drifted in lifeboats for two days. When a freighter picked them up, Tod was clinging to the life ring that now hangs in his shop.

Tod: *"You assume a guilt. Why them, why not me? It weighed on me quite heavily."*

The fatal voyage of the *Albatross* is graphically portrayed in the 1996 Jeff Bridges film *White Squall*.

In the film a tribunal is called, exonerating Tod and the skipper. In real life, that court scene never took place. In the film, Tod plays his own father coming to his defense, something else that never happened in real life.

For Tod, acting in the film was cathartic.

Tod: *"It made up for everything my father never gave me. He never showed any affection or love or respect for me."*

As a consultant on the film, Tod feared opening a Pandora's box of emotion. Instead the movie is helping him shed his albatross.

Tod: *"I feel a lot stronger for getting that monkey off my shoulder. I carried the guilt of [the deaths of] six people. Get rid of that piece of luggage and you feel a lot lighter, more like a hot air balloon."*

Emotion is a powerful creative force, and Tod channels his emotions into his art. He transforms wood and common household objects into amazingly accurate and elegant models of all sorts of ships and schooners. Though his gallery is located right on the harbor in Stonington, he says he is more of a bathtub sailor now. Tod has accomplished a transformation of tragedy into art that is positively Connecticut.

SINCE OUR STORY:

Tod said making the film and seeing his story told on the big screen was "very therapeutic."

Local schools have invited Tod to show the film and talk about his experience. There have been even more requests since the release of the blockbuster movie Titanic.

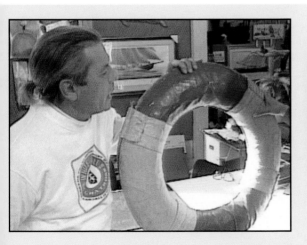

Cemetery Stories

NORWICH

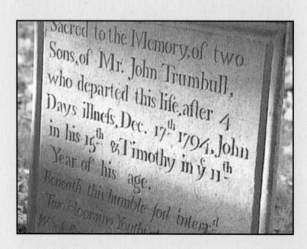

Not all museums have four walls. Some have none. Most of us think of them as graveyards, but if you visit some of Connecticut's ancient burial grounds, you'll learn a lot about the people who lived in the area.

Ruth Brown doesn't find graveyards spooky or creepy. She thinks of them as "open air museums."

Ruth: *"We have art, we have skilled craftsmen. There's history, genealogy, stories."*

You need a guide like Ruth to find one burial ground in eastern Connecticut. Tucked away behind a bank is the old Norwichtown cemetery. Some of the area's first residents have found rest here for nearly three hundred years.

Ruth reads aloud from a tombstone: *"Here lies ye body of Captain Obadiah Smith who died May 11, 1727 and in ye 50th year of his age. Now between these carved stones, which treasure lies, dear Smith his bones."*

Ruth can tell you about the ship captains and soldiers and preachers and mothers and children who lie here, and she can tell you about the carvers who left their marks on the crumbling headstones.

Ruth: *"The important thing on this one is at*

the bottom. It says cut by John Walden of Windham, which is an advertisement to people that wanted a stone similar to that."

Storyteller David Philips says that if you visit on Halloween, you just might meet the ghost of one of Norwich's most infamous residents.

Dave: *"Promptly at midnight, as the churchbells ring the midnight hour, Benedict Arnold, who goes down in history as one of America's greatest traitors and a terrible bad guy, comes to Norwichtown cemetery and visits the grave of his mother, Hannah."*

Dave says Arnold's mother and sisters in Norwich suffered terribly after Arnold was revealed as a traitor and British troops trashed New London. Arnold eventually moved to England, where he is buried.

Dave: *"But I have to believe that anybody, no matter how bad the reputation may be, who returns annually all the way across the ocean, in spirit maybe if not in body, to visit his mother's grave can't be all bad."*

It's a ghost story that's positively Connecticut. ✒

**MORE
GRAVE NEWS:**

Old graveyards abound in Connecticut, and if you think of them, as Ruth does, as open-air museums, they are fascinating. To find out more, you can contact the Connecticut Gravestone Network which offers tours— often in the month of October, the high season for ghosts and cemeteries. Call the network at 860-643-5652, or call your local historical society to find out about the graveyards in your town.

Animal Tales

Raptor Rehabilitators

PORTLAND

W hen I was a kid I tried to rescue starlings when they fell out of their nests to the sidewalks below. I would put them in a shoebox and try to feed them bugs and worms. They never survived. So when I met the Mitchells, I was really impressed. In nearly three decades they saved more than three thousand birds.

The screech of a barn owl is terrifying if you're the mouse this predator is swooping down on. But this particular owl hasn't been hunting since it was injured in an accident. It's being cared for by Janet and Stuart Mitchell, who call their bird hospital the Raptor Hilton. Raptors are birds of prey, and the Mitchells are licensed raptor rehabilitators. About one hundred injured raptors are brought to the Mitchell's home in Portland every year.

Stuart Mitchell: "In the spring we get orphans, no known address, so we can't bring them back to where they should be. So they have to be raised. Later on, during migration, we get impact injuries. Hunting season, we get birds that are shot. The last few years we've seen a lot of poisonings."

The census in the spacious flight cage includes two red-tailed-hawks, a turkey vulture, and a bald eagle with a fused wing. There are ospreys and a variety of owls—some snoozing screech owls, and barred owls with eyes round as marbles.

A horned owl fell out of his nest as a baby.

Diane: *"You actually had to teach this one how to hoot?"*

Janet Mitchell: *"For this bird, what we used to do was play records. We had no adult to teach him, and so what we did was play records or tapes."*

The Mitchells feed their patients some sixty thousand mice a year. Many of the mice are donated by hospitals and universities that are conducting experiments. These are the "clean" mice, from an experiment's control group.

Birds who cannot survive in the wild may stay on with the Mitchells, to be taken to lectures or to serve as surrogate parents for orphans. But the Mitchells' goal is to release recovered birds back into the wild.

Stuart cradles a small owl in his hands and talks to it soothingly: *"We're gonna take you out and let you go."*

The Mitchells gave up reha-bilitating after twenty-eight years because they wanted to travel, and finding a licensed bird-sitter can be a real prob-lem.

One great barred owl that was helped by the Mitchells never really left them. He's nested in their neighborhood for a decade and brings his mate and his young to visit once in a while.

Their proudest moment was the discovery, along the Saint Lawrence Seaway in New York state, of a female bald eagle that they knew very well. Miss Enfield, as they called her, was identified by a band on her leg. The Mitchells had nursed her back to health during an especially rough winter in 1982. Fifteen years later she was banded again, and this time a satel-lite transmitter was attached to her. Wildlife biologists have now traced Miss Enfield to her nesting site near Montreal. Janet Mitchell says all their hard work was worth it, knowing that "we put a few more eagles out there."

First, the owl is banded, weighed, and measured. Then Janet shows me how to hold the tiny fluffy bundle.

Janet: *"If you keep him on his back, he'll stay real quiet. It has a kind of mesmerizing effect."*

It's an incredible feeling to hold a wild creature in your hands, even just for a moment. This saw-whet owl has been with the Mitchells since before Christmas, when he had a run-in with a car. But this is the big day. He's being released. I care-fully place him on a limb of a spruce tree, not far from the flight cage, and tell him: *"You're free ... free to go."*

He hesitates a moment, blinking his big eyes, then tentatively flies away, a few feet at first, then to a higher perch on another tree.

While the Mitchells are saving birds, they say they have a big-ger mission.

Janet: *"Unless we save habitat, unless we do some conserva-tion and some education, then what we're doing doesn't make much sense. Hopefully, people will think about the birds. Someone has to be their advocate."*

That dedication is what makes these raptor rehabilitators positively Connecticut.

Show Biz Dog Trainer

HIGGANUM

I'd heard about Bill Berloni for years, and I was looking for an opportunity to do a story about him. The 20th-anniversary revival of Annie on Broadway was the perfect tie-in.

When Annie belts out "Tomorrow" in the classic Broadway show, there's one man behind the scenes paying more attention to Sandy, the big yellow mutt. He's Bill Berloni of Higganum, who got his start as a theatrical animal trainer twenty years ago in the original production of *Annie* at the Goodspeed Opera House.

Bill: *"I thought I had died and gone to heaven. You know, I'm eighteen years old, an actor, with no professional training, and here I was being offered a part in the show. The director said, 'The only thing you have to do is find and train a dog for no money,' and I said 'Yeah, no problem.'"*

Bill found that first Sandy in the dog pound.

Bill: *"I trained him as you would train your own dog, with love and affection. I figured if he liked the little girl [starring as Annie], he would do anything for her on stage. If he thought the theater was his home, he would be comfortable in it, and that's pretty much the basis of the method I've continued with."*

Today Bill's home is a virtual "Sandy farm,"

where we met Cindy Lou, now starring on Broadway, and her understudies Cosmo, Sparky, and Buster. Each dog speaks on command, as if to introduce themselves. Before stardom these dogs lived a "hard knock life." Cindy Lou was a wild stray, minutes away from being put to sleep.

Bill: *"The warden called me from the pound and he said, 'You know, I got a wild one here, but she's a good looker.' So I went to the dog pound at ten at night and he's there with the needle and he says, 'What do you think,' and well, I say 'Put her in the car.'"*

It may be hard to imagine when you see Bill's pampered little stars, but most of the dogs he works with are rescued animals, dogs that have been caged or neglected, abandoned or even abused.

Two black wirehaired terriers, Max and his understudy Plenty, have just ended their run in the New York production of *Wizard of Oz*, starring comedienne Roseanne as the Wicked Witch. They played Toto. Onstage these dogs have to be highly motivated to act. So Bill forges a bond between the dogs and their human co-stars.

Bill: *"They'll sleep over at the actor's house. The actor will share their lunch with them. They hang out during breaks in rehearsals. So when I release the dog from backstage it's going to someone it really likes."*

Bill's wife, Dorothy, is another former actor. Now she's a trainer too. She puts Plenty through her paces, with the dog dancing on her hind feet atop a picnic table.

Dorothy: *"It's nerve-wracking. It must be like watching your child*

doing a dance recital and you've memorized the little ballet routine that she's supposed to do. Whether she does it or not is another matter."

The Berlonis also act as agents for other people's theatrical pets, negotiating dressing rooms and other perks for their hundreds of clients. But number one in Bill's heart will always be Sandy, the character who became a classic, and turned a young actor into a renowned animal trainer who's positively Connecticut.

MORE DOG TALK:

That big old yellow dog sure opened a lot of doors for Bill Berloni, including the ones to the White House. President Bush's dog Millie was not the first famous dog to write a book. A book written by Sandy, with Bill's help, includes pictures of them with lots of famous people, including more than one president of the United States.

Not long ago a wealthy family in the Hamptons planned a birthday party for their little girl, whose favorite movie is 101 Dalmatians. *They wanted to have 101 Dalmatian puppies at the party, so of course they called Bill to round them up. Well, he didn't come up with 101, but he delivered quite a few. I hear the birthday party was a huge success.*

Cap'n John's Sealwatch

WATERFORD

Captain John Wadsworth often guides his boat, The Sunbeam Express, into Long Island Sound to fish for bass or fluke or bluefish. But in recent years, many trips have had a different goal: wildlife watching.

On a cold day in early spring, no one on board *The Sunbeam Express* is fishing. As the railroad bridge is raised, the hundred-foot-long boat heads out of Waterford, passing New London Ledge Light and the Pequot Lighthouse. We cut between North and South Dumpling Islands and navigate toward Fisher's Island, where we spot the largest colony of harbor seals wintering on the Connecticut coast.

Captain John: *"This is very rich in food here in the wintertime. That's one of the reasons they come south. Believe it or not, this is going south for the winter, for seals."*

Diane: *"Like going to Florida for them!"*

Captain John: *"Yeah, that's right. They enjoy it down here."*

At first they blend into the rocks, but then one by one the seals start to move, and their sleek spotted bodies glide into the Sound. Some stay on their perches, staring back at us.

Captain John started these nature cruises

about five years ago to take up the slack between fishing seasons.

Captain John: *"We were doing some filming, making films for different organizations. When I started telling people what we were doing, they didn't realize we had this wildlife in the area. And so many people expressed a desire to see them that we started the cruises on a limited basis."*

Now John and his son run nature cruises on a regular basis, often taking along an expert from the Mystic Marinelife Aquarium to answer questions.

Nine-year-old Justin Desjardins, of Voluntown, observes the seals carefully and comments: *"They just lay on the rocks all day."*

Diane: *"Doesn't sound like a bad life does it?"*

Justin: *"Nope, and eat fish."*

Captain John: *"Some people come thinking they're going to see a trained animal jumping through hoops and doing some tricks. Those people tend to get a little disappointed. Others are ecstatic over the fact that we have so many animals here in the wild, surviving as well as they do. They just enjoy the fact that they can get out here on a nice day and enjoy nature in the wild."*

The seals stay in Long Island Sound till about the end of May. Just around the time some of us are getting our boats out of storage and heading back into the Sound, they'll be returning to Maine and Nova Scotia. But up until then you can see the seals in their winter retreat that's positively Connecticut.

P.S.:

Captain John's Sunbeam Fleet offers bald-eagle watching from February through March and harbor-seal cruises during April and May. From May through August, he offers whale-watching excursions and lighthouse tours.

Connecticut's Other Huskies

HIGGANUM

If there's one thing I've learned about Connecticut, it's that in spite of its small size, both in geography and in population, you can find just about anything here. A few winters back, when it was snowing twice a week, someone commented to me that the best way to make it through the season would be with a dog sled team. I asked Pat Child, a photographer at Channel 8 who is also a professional dog breeder and show judge, if he knew of any. Sure enough, he pointed me toward some folks who weren't cursing that snowy, snowy winter, but reveling in it.

A chorus of piercing, wolf-like howls fills the air.

On bitter-cold winter days when most dogs and their people are looking for a place to curl up by the fire, Lloyd and Joanne Wyatt's dogs are howling to go out. These Siberian huskies are undaunted by January in Higganum, even when the wind chill is 20 below zero. That's when the Wyatts pack their van with huskies and a dog sled and head into the snow.

Lloyd: *"They're full of energy, they love to do it. When they hear us rattling around the house, they start screaming and they can't wait to go."*

Unloaded at a nearby state park, Kezelkum, Karakum, Kavik, Koriak, and Mira anxiously wait on their gang line. One by one, Joanne and Lloyd hitch them into harnesses attached to their handmade sled.

The team is so pumped, the sled has to be tied to a post to hold the dogs back. Then Joanne hops on the runners, and they're off—with a shout of "Hike!" (not "Mush!"). Another team is soon behind, making tracks through the sunny, snowy fields of Haddam Meadows Park.

Lloyd and Joanne's dogs are used to working as a team.

Joanne: *"They've been together for a number of years, and so they don't fight."*

That doesn't mean dog sledding always goes smoothly.

Joanne: *"You have to be in charge. When you have six dogs and they're in charge, you're in trouble. So I am in charge."*

Diane (laughing): *"But not all the time."*

Joanne laughs too because even an experienced musher can lose her team while trying to turn around. Joanne and the sled disappear from our view for a few minutes, behind a stand of trees. After a couple of minutes, the dogs and sled come hurtling at us, without their driver. Soon Joanne comes trudging back on foot.

Joanne: *"They took off like a shot, dragging me behind them."*

But Joanne comes back laughing, because she and Lloyd are really hooked on running dogs.

Lloyd: *"It's the love of the breed. We're here to use the breed for what they were intended. And you're out there in the fresh air and it's a lot of exercise and it's good for you."*

The Wyatts are active members of the Connecticut Valley Siberian Husky Club and I can see why. After just one ride in the "basket," it's easy to forget about frozen toes and fingers. This season has been a snow bonanza, but when there is no snow the Wyatts resort to sleds with wheels.

Sled dogs. You don't have to head for the Arctic to find them. They're positively Connecticut. 🐾

A FINAL WORD:

About the only thing Joanne and Lloyd like better than running their huskies is introducing other people to the sport. Their club not only holds races that are open to the public, but also offers informal workshops for dog owners who want to try sledding.

Because of the huskies' resemblance to wolves, some people believe they are ferocious, but my photographer on this story, Mark Ciesinksi, has a husky who's afraid of his own shadow. Mark and his wife took their dog to a workshop and found that he loved to pull the sled, but only with Mark's wife on board.

Where the Buffalo Roam

BROOKLYN

arming in Connecticut is a pretty tough proposition. Land values being what they are, many farmers find it more profitable to sell out to developers than to cultivate crops. And the smaller size of Connecticut farms can be a problem, too, making it hard to compete with the vast acreages of farms out West. But some determined farmers are incorporating "agri-tainment" into the mix, inviting tourists to spend time at the farm and to make retail purchases. Austin and Debbie Tanner's farm is a good example of that. And they've got an attraction you don't expect to find in this part of the country, or for that matter in this part of the century.

Buffalo. At one time the Great Plains were black with them. When Columbus landed, there were some 60 million bison on the continent. The Indians revered them. But in the 1800s hunters nearly wiped them out. By the turn of the century, there were as few as two hundred left to roam the United States.

For Brooklyn dairy farmer Austin Tanner and his wife, Debbie, the majestic buffalo embody the romance of American history.

Austin: *"They date back to the beginning of the country. They were here before we were.*

They are just fascinating creatures. There is such a sense of history about them. They are purely American."

Years ago Austin thought that he would like a buffalo as a pet, to keep with his registered Holsteins. Debbie contacted some buffalo experts.

Debbie: *"I called them and they told me how much they wanted for one and they suggested that you should really have two, because they are very social. I decided against that very quickly."*

Instead she gave Austin a membership in the American Bison Association. The association's newsletter led him to an auction, where he promised he was only going to look, not buy.

But Debbie says: *"He came home on a Saturday night and said, 'There are five buffalo coming tomorrow, we should really get ready for them.'"*

Seven years later the herd numbers sixty. During a visit to the Creamery Brook Bison Farm, visitors can bottle-feed Max, a spring bison calf; learn a little bit about dairy farming; maybe even make ice cream the old-fashioned way, by hand-cranking it. Then the Tanners load everyone into the haywagon so you can get up close and personal with their buffalo. The herd in the pasture just beyond the fruit trees is awe-inspiring. These guys are big and wild.

The children in the wagon have a lot to say: *"I think they're mean and they look sort of shabby. They're sort of shaggy, their fur is not very straight."*

A little girl: *"They have bad hairdos."*

Diane: *"What's bad about their hairdos?"*

Girl: *"They're all spiky."*

Their hairdos may be the least of their worries. Some of the bison are headed for the dinner table.

Inside the retail shop, Debbie opens the freezer. *"We have rib steaks, hamburger patties, tenderloin steaks."*

She says the meat is healthful, lower in calories and cholesterol than beef.

Debbie: *"Some people buy it because they know what the meat is. In the grocery store you are not sure where it came from. We only sell our own meat, and we can guarantee that they haven't had any antibiotics or hormones."*

The farm store sells all sorts of buffalo souvenirs, from toys to trinkets to golf balls.

When we come back from our tour, we all enjoy a farm-fresh treat, ice cream hand-cranked by kids. Little Hayden has chocolate, but I have the specialty of the house, bison berry.

Creamery Brook Bison Farm. Preserving a little bit of the old West that's positively Connecticut. 🐾

MORE ON THIS STORY:

Debbie and Austin's farm is now available for children's birthday parties.

WHAT'S COOKING?

The Tanners say buffalo meat can be substituted for beef. But, if you're looking for a more authentic recipe consult Native American Cooking *by Madison author Dale Carson. A member of the Abenaki Nation, Dale has compiled recipes for buffalo, including pot roast, sausage, and stew with roasted barley and onions.*

Eagle Eyes

SOUTHBURY

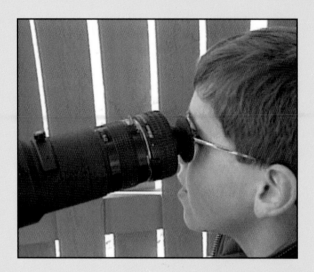

Most of us don't think of Connecticut as a warm place to spend the winter. But, hey, if you hail from northern Maine or Canada, Connecticut seems nearly tropical in January, February, and March. It's not exactly like the swallows returning to Capistrano, but the eagles return annually to Connecticut, and winter is prime time for watching.

They're back! Majestic, soaring high above the Housatonic River, the bald eagles are wintering again near the Shepaug Dam in Southbury.

Lorraine Amalavage volunteers at the observation center operated by Northeast Utilities. A dozen years ago Lorraine was one of the first visitors here, and she fell in love.

Lorraine: *"There's just something awesome about watching a six-foot bird in flight. The maneuverability that these birds have in flight, it's just incredible."*

The eagles migrate here from Maine and Quebec because the living is easy. The operation of the hydroelectric dam keeps the water open, ice free, in spite of the cold. The fish, swimming through the turbines, are stunned and flushed to the surface. Easy pickings in a swoop from a perch nearby.

Josey Oakley is visiting from England.

Josey: *"I've never seen anything like this."*

Kids and adults cluster around the telescopes inside the open-air viewing hut, chattering with excitement.

Lorraine: *"The enjoyment of watching someone's face the first time they see an eagle, you cannot compare that with anything. Especially some of the younger kids."*

Eagles nearly disappeared in the 1960s, but banning the pesticide DDT and passing laws protecting them has helped. At one time this symbol of America was so endangered that there were only four hundred pairs in the continental United States. This winter there may be as many as one hundred eagles in Connecticut alone.

The observation center is a tightly controlled site. If you go to the see the eagles, you'll have to make a reservation. You'll be directed to stay inside the hut, or in the buffer area just outside it, so the eagles are not disturbed.

The observation point is about one thousand feet from the river, where the eagles spend most of their time. If you're lucky you'll see mature eagles crowned in sparkling white, and younger ones, catching fish and eating them in midair.

Dave Rosgen is a wildlife biologist who supervises the site.

Dave: *"Then, if the eagles have eaten sufficiently, had peace and quiet, and it's a nice day, thirty degrees, sunny, thermal updrafts, they do get up and soar and fly back and forth. They play with each other."*

The eagles' stay in Connecticut lasts until mid-March. Lorraine remembers watching them leave for home last year.

Lorraine: *"That was an incredible sight. Seeing twenty-eight birds in the air all at once, and seeing them head out. Knowing that it was spring and they were heading out to their breeding grounds and we would have to wait until next year to see our next eagle."*

Don't wait. This is a winter experience that's positively Connecticut.

> **A REFLECTION:**
>
> *The eagle is our national symbol and we probably take for granted what a beautiful bird it is. We see it all over the place, on postage stamps, in advertisements and textbooks. But see one up close, in flight, and I guarantee you'll feel a chill. I think that's what Lorraine was talking about, enjoying the reaction that people experience. Makes you feel patriotic, and glad our forebears didn't follow Ben Franklin's suggestion and choose the wild turkey as the symbol of America.*

The Oyster Farmer

SOUTH NORWALK

Back when oysters were collected by men in Sharpie sailboats, dozens of oyster companies dotted Connecticut's shoreline. New Haven's Fair Haven section revolved around the oyster trade. Today the oyster business is smaller, but New Haven Harbor is still a setting ground for oysters grown by Hill Bloom.

Hillard and Norman Bloom's company, Tallmadge Brothers, is based in South Norwalk, where they have expanded over the years as other oyster companies have disappeared.

Hill Bloom: *"We started on the sailboats on the natural beds. We dredged oysters under sail when we first got started. And then, oh, about '55 or so, we started in the oyster business ourselves with growing our own oysters."*

Hill remembers the early years were hard.

Hill: *"The hurricanes that started in 1939 and continued through the fifties, they hurt the oyster business. We lost a lot of our inventory then. Of course the pollution, that didn't help it any."*

Hill Bloom harvests thousands of bushels of oysters from Long Island Sound yearly, shipping them all over the country. These are cultivated oysters. The process of raising them is something like underwater farming.

Hill: *"We plant our shells in July, and with good luck, by September we have an oyster set on the shells."*

The shells are planted to attract oyster larvae, which float in the water for several weeks after they're spawned. They'll be moved to deeper water in a few months, where they can winter without danger from storms. They will be moved again to market beds, and when the oysters are four to five years old, dredging boats will scoop them up to be sorted and sold.

Captain Dave Hopp oversees a crew that works twelve hours a day, twelve months a year.

Dave: *"The day goes fairly fast. We have a lot of running time between one area and another and that gives us a lot of time to just sit back and look at the scenery."*

Dave's grandfather was an oysterman.

Dave: *"I was fourteen when I first started on the boat. It was exciting running a boat, and you're your own boss out here."*

Other boats will come out here to battle starfish, the oyster's worst enemy in the Sound now that pollution is under control.

Hill: *"Connecticut has really cleaned up its harbors. So the oyster business, I think, is on the comeback."*

Today Connecticut oysters are considered among the best in the country, with a nice hard shell, good fat meat, and a sweet taste.

My grandfather told me he figured the first man who ever ate a raw oyster had to be either crazy or starving. Well, these days you don't have to be either to enjoy this delicacy, but it does help to be here, because oystering is positively Connecticut.

A LITTLE MORE:

Oysters were a staple in the diets of native Americans who lived along the coast and of pre–Revolutionary War Colonial Americans. Oyster farming is said to have started on Long Island Sound in the 1700s. In the late 1800s Norwalk was known as the oyster capital of the nation.

Are there pearls in Connecticut oysters? According to Hill Bloom, once in a while a small black pearl shows up in an oyster, but it has no value. Jewelry-quality pearls come from cultivated pearl oysters.

Guiding Lights

BLOOMFIELD

The Fidelco Guide Dog Foundation trains about fifty dogs a year, but hopes to increase that to one hundred. The demand for dogs is rising because so many more people who are blind are now able to join the workforce, thanks to new technologies like talking computers.

Mary Hook lost her eyesight five years ago, the result of diabetes.

Mary: *"Before I got Nemo I was really dependent on people and I couldn't even go to the store by myself. I couldn't do anything."*

Nemo is Mary's guide dog—born, bred, and trained in Bloomfield by Fidelco. Nemo is from a line of German shepherds established by industrialist Charles Kaman thirty years ago.

Charles: *"The difficulty is to get steady nerves, animals that are secure, that are at peace. I've called it the mentality of an astronaut."*

Kaman is known worldwide for building helicopters and guitars, but perhaps closest to his heart is the Fidelco Guide Dog Foundation, which he and his wife supervise. Their vision is shared by dozens of foster families who raise Fidelco puppies. Each puppy goes to a temporary foster home when it is about eight weeks old.

Susan Volhart and her family are teaching manners to Dijon, and getting her used to strange people, new places, even cats. In October the Volharts will return Dijon to Fidelco for training.

Susan: *"We'll miss her because she's really become a close part of the family. But when I think about where she's going and what she's going to do, she's really going to start her life there."*

Fidelco breeds these German shepherds specially for the work they will eventually have to do.

Trainer John Byfield: *"They're compact, and take short steps rather than long steps. They have nice strong backs, and good hips and feet."*

The shepherds go to school for six months to learn to guide their blind owners. Working their way through obstacle courses, they learn to gauge their owner's height so they can skirt barriers on the streets.

John: *"They have to learn to get across the street, come back to the curb, being careful to go around manhole covers and other things. In some situations we are totally surprised because we have never run into them ourselves, and yet the dogs are able to think them through and proceed safely."*

Guide dogs like Nemo have opened new doors for people like Mary Hook, and people like Mary have opened a new world for the man who got it all started, Charles Kaman.

Charles: *"I see them from time to time, and I try not to let the tears show, but it's a very human and moving experience to see someone move forward in life."*

That's what makes the Fidelco Guide Dog Foundation positively Connecticut. 🐾

MORE GOOD NEWS:

Nemo was named guide dog of the year by a national organization for the dramatic way he improved Mary's life. Another Fidelco dog, Karl, was guide dog of the year in 1997 for changing George Salpietro's life. George went blind at forty and gave up an active career and traveling all over the world, to sit in a rocking chair at home. Then he was paired with Karl, and now they both travel.

As a vice president of Fidelco, George gives hundreds of speeches every year to educate people about blindness and about guide dogs.

Fidelco dogs that are not suited for guiding the blind are often donated to other service agencies. The state police love them, and one has gone as far away as Alaska, where he works as a search and rescue dog.

Talent Show

House Painters

OLD LYME

F rom the turn of the century until Florence Griswold's death in 1937, her home in Old Lyme was also home to a colony of artists. Some of the greatest American impressionists literally left their marks throughout her house.

Florence Griswold ran a boarding house with a difference. Her boarders were some of the most renowned artists of their time, creating a style of art known as American impressionism. The elegant Georgian-style house is now a museum.

Jeffrey Andersen, the museum's director, explained what drew them here.

Jeffrey: *"They very much loved the landscape and the sense of place that this corner of Connecticut and New England has with all of its low-lying river areas."*

Even as a museum, the building has the atmosphere of someone's private home—but with a very special distinction.

Jeffrey: *"One of the really unusual features of the house itself are these door panels which you see throughout the building. They were painted by the artists who lived here and worked in the studios out back."*

The dozens of boarders who stayed here over the years left Miss Florence with doors and a dining room that are priceless. Some

of the most celebrated American impressionists left their marks, including Childe Hassam, Willard Metcalf, and Guy Wiggins. But one artist's work is no longer on view. He made the mistake of moving out without paying his bill.

Jeffrey: *"So the others decided they would remove his panel painting. They turned it over and William Chadwick, another member of the colony, painted on the reverse."*

Not content to leave just their artwork, they left their likenesses, too, on a panel featuring two half-empty bottles. And what was in the bottles?

Jeffrey: *"Mastic, which is something they used to prepare canvases, and [in the other bottle] rye whiskey, used, I guess, to prepare themselves. You can see the Griswold house in the background and this really is a delightful narrative or story of the artists on this imaginary fox hunt."*

The Connecticut landscape first drew the artists to Florence Griswold's home, but once they got there, they memorialized the house, its mistress, and her property, painting images of the gardens, the barn, even Miss Florence's handyman.

Debbie Fillos, curator of the museum, has a good idea why Florence ran the boarding house for over three decades.

Debbie: *"She really did it out of generosity and love of the artists. But I don't think she was necessarily the best business manager and probably never charged as much room and board as she should have. She would get by through selling Colonial American furniture out of the front hall of her home. She also used the front hall as a gallery for the works by many of the artists."*

Those artists eventually turned her whole house into a permanent gallery, and a monument to art that is positively Connecticut. 🖋

Florence Griswold must have loved seeing her house decorated for Christmas. After all, it was her birthday, too. My favorite time to visit is during the Celebration of Holiday Trees. A volunteer committee begins planning the decorations a year ahead. The ornaments on lavishly decorated trees complement the furnishings in each room and their colors are sometimes plucked from the palette of the artist whose work hangs nearby. My favorite is a tree that looks like it's dusted with new-fallen snow. It's actually wired with thousands of blossoms of Queen Anne's Lace that volunteers clip during the summer and then dry for winter.

The museum has bought more than four acres of land along the Lieutenant River, behind Miss Florence's house. That acquisition means that most of her original twelve-acre estate is intact again. A 1998 archaeological dig uncovered remnants of the Lyme Art Colony. There are plans to replant Miss Florence's gardens and apple orchard, which inspired so many wonderful paintings.

The Music Man

The great Irving Berlin wrote a show for the troops that kept them applauding in the darkest hours of World War II. A Chester man had the thrill of being part of it all.

Surely every soldier could relate to the lyrics of one particular song, penned by Irving Berlin for *This Is the Army,* the musical he wrote as a gift to the adopted country he loved so much:

"Oh how I hate to get up in the morning, oh how I'd love to remain in bed."

Max Showalter, now of Chester, was part of the all-military cast of *This Is the Army* sent by Irving Berlin to entertain troops all over the globe. Max was discovered by Berlin while Max was attached to the Army Entertainment Division at Camp Kilmer, New Jersey. Berlin caught Max in an impromptu performance at a New York nightclub, playing the piano and singing. The next day Max was summoned by his commander and told that Berlin wanted him to audition for *This Is the Army.*

Max remembers that fateful meeting with Berlin.

Max: *"He said, 'I think it would be ideal if you came along with the show.' And he*

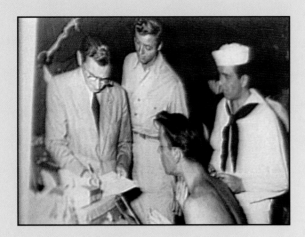

Max left Hollywood in 1984 for Chester, a town he had visited years earlier when he appeared in the Doris Day film It Happened to Jane, *which was shot there. He came back to Connecticut to stage* Harrigan and Hart, *the musical he composed.*

Max was a protégé of Oscar Hammerstein and appeared in fifteen musicals, fifty-four films, and more than one thousand TV shows. He has such wonderful anecdotes about the greats of Hollywood and Broadway that, for a while whenever a star passed away, we would invite Max on the air to reminisce. Eventually, after the deaths of Rock Hudson and several other stars within a short period of time, Max pleaded, "Why don't you call me when someone is born?"

After more than 50 years in show business, Max is now trying to establish the Max Showalter Foundation to house his remarkable theater library and his extensive collection of film, music, and theater memorabilia. He wants his collection to be available to the young artists that he nurtures so generously in Connecticut.

said, 'What we'll do is get you a special piano and you'll be able to play in all the hospitals where we play,' and he said, 'Would you like to go?' Then I thought, 'Well, I'm going to see what I can do,' and I said, 'I would love to go Mr. Berlin, if you would write a song for me to sing.' And he said, 'Well, I think that can be done.'"

Max sang that song—"Kick in the Pants"—in England, Ireland, Italy, Egypt, and North Africa in a two-and-a-half-year world tour. The Allies' enemies Japan and Germany were the butt of this tune, which ended with these words:

"The happy ending catch 'em bending
Do the kick
Do the kick in the pants!"

Max: "Eisenhower said later, at the Palladium, 'Well you're the greatest morale builders we have.' And because of this, Berlin Sally was really out to get us. . . . And so everywhere we went, when we played in Italy or wherever we played, we'd find time bombs in the theater."

But you know the old-show business chestnut: The show must go on! Max remembers a performance in Italy.

Max: "The German planes came over that night, and they had to shut off all the electricity. And the boys then in the audience turned their flashlights on the stage so we could perform. In the Philippines there were snipers who were sniping at the stage while we performed!"

In his fifty-year stage, film, and recording career, Max (who was known as Casey Adams for ten years) performed with the biggest stars of Hollywood and Broadway. Personally inscribed photos of many of them line the walls of his Chester home. Max treasures the wartime letter Irving Berlin wrote to his folks back in Kansas, letting them know their son overseas was doing just fine, and doing his part.

Max Showalter—a music man who is positively Connecticut. ✒

The Woodworking Wedgwood Twins

KILLINGWORTH

I'm always getting phone calls from people who would like me to do a story about a fundraiser for their church or their school or their pet project. I'd always like to help out, but the problem is how to make it interesting. I'll ask them if there is anything unusual about the event, trying to find an angle that would make a great story.

One time I got a call about a Congregational Church auction in Killingworth. I asked the minister the usual questions. He knew just what I meant. "We do have one really, really fine piece of handmade furniture," he said. Then he told me about the men who made it.

Working hand in hand comes naturally to John and Jim Wedgwood. The identical twins are seventy-six years old, and they have almost never been apart. Jim and John live in Killingworth together, eat every meal together, even served together in the military. Still, they don't have much to say on the subject of their relationship.

Diane: *"Do you guys ever disagree?"*
Jim: *"We don't have too much trouble."*
Diane: *"Ever get tired of each other?"*
John: *"No."*

They'd rather concentrate on making furniture. It's a passion the twins share. They started making furniture after they retired from similar jobs in state parks.

John: *"I got sick of hanging around."*

So they outfitted their barn with an array of tools and a supply of cherry wood and bought some books on early American antiques. But how do they fashion furniture just by poring over pictures in books?

Jim: *"I don't know. You just go ahead and do it. That's all, just do it."*

The Wedgwoods make it sound simple, when in fact they are creating near-museum-quality reproductions, like an elaborate desk or a bonnet-top highboy.

Their friend Bruce Campbell, an attorney, has collected some of their work.

Bruce: *"They're modest master craftsmen who are not at all impressed that they can do what they do. They're a team all the way. They operate like a fine machine."*

The Wedgwoods don't sell their furniture, though they do sometimes give it away. They contributed one piece for the church auction in Killingworth.

The twins say if they sold their furniture, they'd have to keep to a schedule and might not be able to choose the projects they want to work on.

John: *"I wouldn't want to do custom work. I wouldn't like that, and I think I'd be hard to live with."*

Hard to live with? Not for his brother, who has lived with him for three-quarters of a century. The Wedgwoods, putting their stamp on fine furniture that's positively Connecticut. ✒

THE REST OF THE STORY:

I mentioned that their friend Bruce Campbell has collected some of the Wedgwoods' furniture. They brought one piece to Campbell's house as a "hostess gift" on Thanksgiving. Most people would have brought a pie. Now those are the kind of guests to invite for a holiday!

Bubblemania

EAST HADDAM

Casey Carle is a clown, a performer, an artist, a scientist, and a teacher. A pretty interesting package. He's also a bubble-ologist. What's that? It's a person who takes the simple elements of nature and turns them into a show that has kids and adults ooohing and aaahing, and wondering how he did it. Best part is, he tells them.

Most artists hope their work will last for posterity. Not Casey Carle. His art is ephemeral. He makes sculpture from soap bubbles.

Casey: *"They're there. You enjoy them and then they're gone, and part of what makes them so mesmerizing is that the beauty is temporary. Which is fortunate, because if they didn't pop I'd have to have a much bigger house to put everything in."*

In performing 250 shows a year, Casey never gets tired of the ooohs and aaahs and applause as he creates spaceships, a crystal ball, square bubbles, even bubbles inside bubbles. But Casey sees more in his bubbles than beauty. He sees science. And when the East Haddam man performs his show "Bubblemania" for school groups, they get a healthy dose of science.

Casey: *"I love taking something that is identifiable already—that is, the soap bubble—and* *turning it into something extraordinary. And explaining that it's the knowledge of science that is allowing me to do what they see as magic."*

Casey began entertaining with bubbles as a clown in the Ringling Brothers Barnum & Bailey Circus.

Casey: *"I was told by senior clowns that everything had been done already, nothing was new. And I took that to heart. I decided to try a medium that was different. Seeing how large bubbles affected me, I thought if I could combine that sense of awe with pratfalls and comedy in the center ring,* that *would be entertainment."*

Casey hopes that combining science with entertainment will convince his audiences, like the one at St. Gabriel's School in Milford, that science is creative and imaginative.

Jay Judge (a sixth-grader): *"I thought it was interesting and funny and he had a lot of good stuff to tell us about."*

Brother Gerald (principal): *"These kids learned all the way through the assembly, and I don't think they knew it."*

Casey coaxes his creations from bubble molds crafted from string, coat hangers, and soda can rings. He makes teeny tiny bubbles, and gigantic bubbles.

Casey shares a bubbleologist's secret with the kids: He adds glycerin to make them last longer.

Casey: *"That helps on days when the humidity is low, but on high-humidity days you don't even need that. It's a matter of knowing when to make the bubbles as well, and what they like and don't like. Bubbles are kind of finicky about certain things."*

All of which Casey Carle knows well, because after all he is a bubbleologist mixing art and science in a combination that is positively Connecticut. ✦

ALL IN THE FAMILY:

Casey met his wife, Kandie, when she was an elephant rider in the circus. They like to say they ran away from the circus together. She now performs as the "Victorian Lady" for audiences ranging from school children to senior citizens.

Kandie starts her show dressed in prim Victorian corset and bloomers. As she dresses, she uses each article of clothing to tell the story of how people lived.

Kandie's love for the history and romance of the Victorian era was passed on to her, along with some of her costumes, by her grandmother and great-grandmother. She says: "If they were alive today they would be thrilled that I am doing all of this and keeping part of history alive."

The Troubador

NORTH GUILFORD

*C*onnecticut is alive with music and musicians. *Recognizing the place music plays in our lives, the state Commission on the Arts bestows a special honor on one musician each year, who is named state troubadour. We caught up with one of these troubadours, Phil Rosenthal, during a performance at a library with his family band.*

"Mama don't allow no bass playing round here." These lyrics, along with strains of bluegrass music, are heard through the stacks of the library.

Phil Rosenthal and his wife, Beth Sommers Rosenthal, have been making music together for twenty years. But these days their songs sound different. That's because their kids, fifteen-year-old Naomi and twelve-year-old Daniel, are performing with them.

Phil: *"When we play in our family band, it's probably the most fun."*

Beth: *"It's the best band I've been in, I think. The kids are just so talented, they left me in the dust last year."*

Daniel adds a jazz influence with his trumpet, and Naomi's flute and voice have filled out their sound. Naomi sings in a rock band, too.

Naomi: *"My friends like the fact that my dad*

has a recording studio because then we get to make tapes."

Daniel: *"I want to be a professional trumpet player when I grow up, so this is my first break."*

There are some downsides to a family band, though.

Naomi: *"Every chance we get, we have to keep practicing these songs that I've been hearing since I was little. So while other people might enjoy them, I get sick of them."*

These days Phil is on a mission to spread music throughout Connecticut as the official state troubadour. And what exactly is that?

Phil: *"Well, people have asked me that. They say, now does that mean we might see you on our local green, riding a pony and playing a song on your mandolin?"*

Probably not. Phil sees his mission as state troubadour as furthering music in Connecticut by recording local artists and creating a state archive of their music.

Since the addition of Daniel and Naomi, the Sommers Rosenthal Family Band has expanded its repertoire beyond its folk and bluegrass roots. Naomi likes to sing the blues, and Daniel has continued his interest in jazz and the trumpet. Now sixteen, he leads the Daniel Rosenthal Jazz Quartet, playing his own compositions. Daniel is especially interested in the fusion of jazz and klezmer, a music style popular among Eastern European Jews.

Besides Phil's responsibilities as state troubadour and the family's performances together as a band, Phil and Beth are busy running their record company. American Melody Records specializes in children's recordings. Their tapes and CDs feature kids' stories, plus music in bluegrass and traditional folk styles. Phil says there's now a glut of music for kids, but not all of it is good.

Phil: *"A lot of people who have gotten into it sound like people who maybe shouldn't be in music. They couldn't cut it in other kinds of music, so they figured, 'Well I can do kids' music, you know. You don't have to be great for that.' But if anything, I think the opposite is true."*

That's why Phil and Beth and their children are so intent on creating high-quality music for their audience of children and their parents. And that's why Phil Rosenthal was named state troubadour, a post that's positively Connecticut. ♪

SINCE OUR STORY:

1998's state troubadours are Jeff and Synia McQuillan, who use African drums and chanting to weave what they call "Tales from the First World." Their stories are from Africa and the Caribbean, and some are from here at home. They incorporate Connecticut history into their songs, too, like Jeff's song inspired by the Indian word for Connecticut, which means "long river."

It goes like this:
"From Portland down to Haddam's Neck,
The memories like an old ship wreck,
Even though the body's gone,
The river hums a gospel song
Long long river ..."

Krikko's Big Idea

NEW HAVEN

My friend, news photographer George DeYounge, had been telling me about Krikko for months. But I just didn't get it. It wasn't until I met Krikko and saw his artwork that I realized why George had been so enthusiastic. Gregory Krikko Obbott is from Nigeria. He's an architect, but he hasn't been able to pursue that career in this country. But he is using his skill, talent, and education to create something else, and he's probably going to make a ton of money doing it.

At first glance, Gregory Krikko Obbott's *Super Big Apple* appears to be a photograph taken from a helicopter. But get closer, and you begin to notice the strokes and shadings from the 2,500 pencils he used up in creating this monumental drawing of Manhattan and its buildings, down to the finest detail.

Krikko: *"Drawing one building and then moving from that building to the next one you almost have to reinvent yourself to be that designer. I am very inspired. I can see the entire picture in my mind before I start drawing it."*

Krikko started *Super Big Apple* while he was still living in Africa. He completed it four years later in New Haven, where he now lives and works. It is gargantuan: twenty feet high and fifteen feet wide.

If you ever have a chance to see a Krikko drawing up close, you'll probably want to do what I did: Climb a ladder and get up close so you can look for something that's familiar. I found Saint Patrick's Cathedral, and right down the street was the building where my dad worked for years and years. It's only one of ten thousand buildings Krikko sketched, after consulting maps and photos and counting actual floors and windows.

Krikko: *"It's got to be accurate. Otherwise they say, 'Oh, that's not the way it is.'"*

He's even planning updates to the Manhattan drawing, as new buildings are erected.

Krikko: *"It's not easy to create this stuff. If you're going to wait for a commission, then you might never do it. So the thing is, get started. If you have an idea, get started."*

He's now working on *Windy City,* his rendition of Chicago, which will be four times as big as *Super Big Apple.* I asked how he can wrap his mind around such a vast project.

Krikko: *"Just keep on going. Kind of take one step at a time and don't ever think of giving up."*

He works twelve hours a day, stopping occasionally to take a run or play his saxophone.

While planning his next projects, renderings of Sydney and San Francisco, Krikko is also at work on a familiar landscape, his new hometown, New Haven. Krikko is capturing a bird's-eye view that's positively Connecticut. 🖋

P.S.:

You may have to hunt to find an exhibit of Krikko originals. Few museums can devote that much space to one piece of art. But because people have been so enthralled by his monolithic pieces, he has made scaled-down posters of Super Big Apple, which are selling well in New York City. He hopes to translate that success into calendars, umbrellas, T-shirts, and other merchandise.

Campus Classics

NORWICH

Only two fine-art museums in the United States are located on a high school campus. One is at Philips Academy in Andover. The other is at Norwich Free Academy.

Walk into the main gallery of this eastern Connecticut museum and you may wonder for a moment if you're at the Louvre in Paris. Or the Vatican in Rome. Or the Parthenon in Athens. But you're actually in the Slater Museum at Norwich Free Academy. And you're not looking at original works of art—not the *Pieta* by Michelangelo, or Donatello's *David*. They are simply plaster cast replicas of some of the world's greatest pieces of sculpture.

Mary-Anne Hall, the museum's curator of education, explains how the 150 replicas were created.

Mary-Anne: *"They would make molds from the original pieces. They would have to rub the surface of the original. Today you wouldn't be allowed to do such a thing."*

Just before the turn of the century, it was quite popular for museums to acquire collections of plaster casts. A delegation from the Metropolitan Museum of Art in New York came to Norwich to see this collection and promptly ordered one of its own. But in the early 1920s casts fell out of fashion. Many museums got rid of their collections in favor of buying and displaying original works. The Norwich Free Academy collection is now regarded as one of the best of its kind in the world.

The museum is named for John Fox Slater, a textile magnate, who was Norwich's wealthiest citizen and a trustee of the Academy. For one hundred years this museum has been a classroom to Academy students with the casts an integral part of their studies of the classics.

Mary-Anne: *"When students study Greek mythology or they study the Periclean Age, the visual aids are literally these casts. The whole class will come over, we talk about things that they know, and I give them a lecture based on the casts."*

The museum's collection has diversified over the years. It now includes original works of art from Japan, early American furniture, and native American art, all of which are incorporated into history, literature, and social studies courses.

Taking classes in a museum inspires some students at the Academy to "major" in art, studying with artists like museum director Joseph Gualtieri. Sixty years of Gualtieri's paintings hang in the museum's Converse Gallery. When we visited he was leading a painting class through there.

An Academy graduate, Joseph Gualtieri is an inspiration to the art students today.

The Slater Museum, a Norwich landmark that's positively Connecticut. 🖋

A FINAL WORD:

The Norwich Free Academy is an independent school, neither a public school nor a private school. Students from eight towns—Bozrah, Canterbury, Franklin, Lisbon, Preston, Norwich, Sprague, and Voluntown—can attend the Academy. The towns, in effect, pay tuition for their students who attend. It is one of the few high schools in the nation where a student can major in art.

Poet of the Ferry

ESSEX

Many of us like our jobs. Some of us even love our jobs. But Rick Lyon is so moved by where he works and the place he lives that he writes poetry about it. Visit Rick Lyon at work, and you may feel poetic too.

Somehow, Rick Lyon always knew that one day he would captain the little canopied ferry that carries people back and forth from the Essex Island Marina to the foot of Ferry Street. The ferry makes the tiniest of voyages—a trip of barely eighty feet.

Rick: *"My dad had that job, back in the thirties, when it was just a little rowboat taking people ashore, and he has his stories, too."*

Shuttling passengers all day is not the solitary life one imagines a poet would lead.

Rick: *"No matter how much you're interested in what's on the page, and language, life is what it's about."*

Rick is drawn to the water, and to its creatures.

In his poem "Gulls" he writes:
"The fish get the bugs and the birds get the fish
and nobody gets the birds because there's a law against it.
The gulls act almost as if they know that."

Some of his poetry pays tribute to the

people who live along the Connecticut River.

Rick reads from the title piece in a book of his poetry, *Bell 8*. The poem takes its title from the bell buoy two miles from the mouth of the river.

"Old man Spring was poor but kind.

The boat he lived on, all these years, is on the bottom now.

He died, and then it sank,

though they'd have happily gone down together."

Carol Wallace of Old Saybrook is a passenger on the ferry.

Carol: *"I know just what he's talking about. Who lived on what boat, and about how things have changed from the way the town and the people used to be."*

To those of us who just visit here, Essex may seem like the "town that time left behind," with all its antique homes and quaint charm. But to Rick Lyon, his adopted hometown has changed a lot.

"Bell 8" laments the gentrification of Essex. Rick reads:

"The hardware store's gone, too, displaced by rising rents,

and our grocer's upcoming retirement might bring another clothing shop.

The town grows more and more exclusive,

with grander mansions, finer views, underscoring what's lost."

Others prefer to see what Essex has gained. Gail Scherer is a business-woman in town, who happens to be riding the ferry.

Diane (to Gail): *"There are a lot of tourist attractions and things that people find enchanting about Essex. Think Rick could be added to the list?"*

Gail: *"Absolutely, he's number one. He's our only poet that I know of."*

A poet who has traveled some, and found the road that leads home. In his poem called "Roads," Rick writes:

"The main road's the same one called by another name—

in Essex, it's the Saybrook road; in Saybrook, the Essex road—

it's what you're oriented towards."

Rick Lyon is oriented toward Long Island Sound and the river. That's what makes his poetry positively Connecticut. 🎣

MORE ABOUT RICK:

He's returned home to Essex after another journey across the United States and Europe. Bell 8 is in its second printing. His next book of poetry, Notre Dame de Bon Voyage ("Our Lady of Good-byes"), was written in the wake of the breakup of a great romance. Although the poems were written in Europe, they too have a fla-vor of the sea, since they were composed in places like the French Riviera and the Greek isles.

Movie Memories

MIDDLETOWN

There's a bit of Hollywood here in Connecticut. It's the Wesleyan Cinema Archives, where the personal collections of important actors and directors are treasured and preserved.

The Wesleyan Cinema Archives building looks like something out of a Frank Capra movie—the kind of house where George Bailey lived in the film *It's a Wonderful Life.* In a way, Bailey does live here, because this is the house where Capra's legacy lives on.

Just one shelf in the vault is enough to make film buffs salivate. There are Capra's own editions of *Mr. Smith Goes to Washington, You Can't Take It With You,* and my favorite, *It's A Wonderful Life,* which shows that the movie originally had a different beginning.

Curator Jeanine Basinger: *"It was set in heaven, in Benjamin Franklin's office. A lot of famous characters, political characters, were standing around talking, and they were asked to come down and help George Bailey with his problem."*

Instead, Capra decided on something else.

Jeanine: *"He went into the far more visual and simple method of just having the twinkling talking stars briefly at the beginning. And I think that was a very good idea."*

Other directors have donated their collections, too, including Martin Scorsese, Federico Fellini, John Waters, and Clint Eastwood.

Elia Kazan's notes on directing *A Streetcar Named Desire* are here, including a notation that Marlon Brando's apartment had no telephone.

There are treasures such as the Oscar Ingrid Bergman won in 1944 for her performance in *Gaslight*. Associate Curator Leith Johnson says an early scrapbook shows Bergman always knew what she wanted.

Leith: *"As early as age nine she was already before the camera in a costume, in a performance, knowing exactly what she wanted to do."*

There's the Ingrid Bergman captured on film, in classics like *Casablanca*, and the Ingrid Bergman curator Jeanine Basinger has come to know.

Jeanine: *"Ingrid Bergman's collection reveals her to be a woman who married and had children. She loves her children, she has many many snapshots and photos of her children. It shows her to be a human being as well as an actress."*

Looking through Bergman's personal and professional mementos is a little like rifling someone's attic. There's the Swedish passport that belonged to the four-year-old Ingrid, and her diary. It details her appearance at fifteen years of age in a play called *Green Elevator*. She writes of the audience: "They loved me."

The archives also contain scrapbooks of 1930s screen star Kay Francis.

Jeanine: *"When you look at a book like this, you see someone who is at the very peak, at the very top, and then it was over. So you are able to see a career emerge, grow, hit the top, and then fall off, so you have a complete story of stardom."*

The collection reveals the challenges faced by even the biggest stars.

Jeanine: *"Take a look at Clint Eastwood's report card, and they say, 'Oh boy, he's a nice young man, but he can't act, he can't sing, he can't dance.'"*

Jeanine hopes that report inspires young people who study Eastwood's development as a film star and acclaimed director.

Also in the archives: the pink satin dress imprinted with giant cockroaches that Ricki Lake wore to the prom in the John Waters film *Hairspray*.

Jeanine: *"There's no one like John Waters. There's no one like him as a filmmaker, there's no one like him as a person, or a writer. Every time I see that roach dress, I think this sums up John Waters."*

The Wesleyan Cinema Archives—a little bit of Hollywood that's positively Connecticut.

A CLOSER LOOK:

The archive is not a museum but a place for the serious study of film. Jeanine says, "You learn how it really was, how the business worked, what the social attitudes were, what the working attitudes were, and how films got made and for what reasons." The archive is not generally open to the public but is accessible to scholars.

The Joy of Eating

The First American Cookbook

WEST HARTFORD

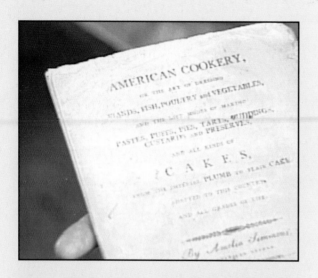

*I*magine trying to cook without your microwave, without your Crock-Pot, without your electric or gas oven. Imagine trying to make an entire meal for a family over an open fire in a fireplace with cast iron pans. There are people who actually do this all the time at some of the historic homes sprinkled throughout Connecticut. The woman who created the blueprint for how to do this the right way, the woman who wrote the very first American cookbook, did her historic work right here in Connecticut. We had an opportunity to try one of her recipes.

At the Noah Webster house in West Hartford, Sally Whipple is cooking the old-fashioned way—the really old-fashioned way.

Sally: *"In Colonial cooking you can cook a lot of ways, but the way we're going to do it today is by taking the hot coals out of the fire and putting them down on the hearth. This would be the equivalent to a burner on your stove today."*

This is the way Amelia Simmons cooked when she wrote the first American cookbook, in 1796, according to Diana McCain of the Connecticut Historical Society.

Diana: *"Right on the title page she calls her-*

self an American orphan. Most women would have learned this from their mothers, but she wrote it for others like herself who had not had anyone to teach them."

American Cookery was the first cookbook with recipes using native American ingredients, like corn and pumpkins, foods they didn't have in Europe. It became a best seller. Still, cooking in those days was no picnic, as we learned watching Sally make mushroom fricassee.

Sally: *"It's really hard to regulate the heat. You can't put it on high or put something on 375 degrees."*

As the mushrooms and onions sauté, Sally adds egg yolks seasoned with spices that would have been grown in a Colonial kitchen garden. This dish would not have been common in the Noah Webster household. When the dictionary author was growing up, this was a working farm, and most meals were simple affairs.

Sally steps into the open hearth of the fireplace and lifts a long-handled tool with a basket on the end that clutches a slice of bread. She moves it a few inches closer to the fire.

Sally: *"I've got toast cooking. Time to flip it over."*

We tasted the mushroom fricassee, eating as they would have in those days, off a broad-blade knife, not with a fork. Manners have changed.

The Webster house seems an appropriate place to explore this first American cookbook. Noah Webster wrote the first dictionary that defined the American version of the English language, while Amelia Simmons made the break from English cooking to a new American style. Two books that declared our independence, and are positively Connecticut. 🐚

WHAT ELSE IS COOKING:

Some typical recipes in American Cookery *are for Indian slapjack and for Johnny cake. Amelia's recipe for Johnny cake reads like this: "Scald one pint of milk and put to three pints of indian meal and one half pint of flour. Bake before the fire." Reprints of the cookbook are available through the Connecticut Historical Society in Hartford.*

Randall's (Extra) Ordinary

NORTH STONINGTON

Wood smoke drifts through the air outside Randall's Ordinary. Inside, the fire is being stoked up to cook lunch. In their colonial dress, Cindy and Bill Clark are caretakers of history in North Stonington.

Cindy and Bill Clark's 300-year-old house was built by John Randall, a farmer from England who came over in the 1600s. Randall was an Anabaptist who helped found North Stonington after a religious disagreement with Stonington's Puritan minister. A later Randall, William, fought in the War of 1812. Darius, the last Randall to own the property, saw action in the Civil War and is thought to have hidden escaped slaves in the root cellar.

The house is now an ordinary, the seventeenth-century term for tavern and inn. However, Randall's Ordinary is anything but. The Clarks cook pre-Revolutionary War recipes the old-fashioned way.

Cindy: *"We gather hot embers from the fire and we are really creating a burner right on the stone hearth with all the red-hot embers. And that's where the term open-hearth cooking applies, because what we've done is come right out on the open hearth and created a burner."*

Most of the firewood is chopped on their twenty-seven-acre property.

Cindy is baking spider bread, named for the cast iron pot it's made in, with its long spindly legs. She's careful as she moves along the hearth, preparing the meal.

Cindy: *"Clothing fires were the second leading cause of death among Colonial women, after childbirth."*

The Clarks' passion for collecting antique cookware and cookbooks led them here.

Bill: *"A good part of it comes from coming out of the sixties, where Cindy didn't want to be the little lady in the kitchen while I was out in the living room entertaining everybody. So with hearth cooking, everybody's in the same room laughing, having a drink together, and having a good time."*

Lunch is served à la carte and features colonial favorites such as deep dish chicken pie or sautéed Nantucket scallops. Dinner is a fixed-price meal of either meat, fish, or fowl such as goose roasted on a spit and served with red cabbage and apples. The taproom offers eighteenth-century libations such as port, ale, Madeira wine, and hot spiced cider. You can finish with a dessert Martha Washington might have made, like bird's-nest pudding, an apple baked in custard and stuffed with golden raisins and nuts.

Like a true colonial tavern, Randall's Ordinary offers more than food and spirits. They have lodging, too. There are three rooms in the main house, and an antique hay barn relocated from upstate New York has nine rooms. The renovated barn also boasts a suite in the silo, with a Jacuzzi tub set beneath a skylight view of the starriest skies in Connecticut.

Bill: *"I call it monument building. We've inherited a heritage and our job is to use it and pass it on and to be part of history. I think history is very much a living thing."*

It's that reverence for history and the way the Clarks live it that makes Randall's Ordinary positively Connecticut.

MORE ABOUT THIS STORY:

Bill and Cindy Clark opened Randall's Ordinary in 1987, one hundred years after the Randalls sold the farm. Cindy learned Colonial cooking techniques through lessons at Old Sturbridge Village. Their recipes were gleaned from antique cookbooks, including Amelia Simmons' American Cookery, the very first American cookbook, which was published in Connecticut in 1796.

The Clarks sold Randall's Ordinary to the Mashantucket Pequot tribal nation in 1995. Except for adding two oxen and some other farm animals, innkeepers Bill and Diane Foakes say they don't intend to change Randall's much, just preserve it. They do plan to move an eighteenth-century house to the property and rebuild it piece by piece.

Teatime

ELLINGTON

A growing trend in eating out these days is a meal most Americans have never had on the menu: tea. It's a throwback to another time that's fitting in just fine at a tearoom in Ellington.

In Victorian times in jolly old England, time stood still in the afternoon as people sat down for the meal known as tea. Jo Medycki has never been to England, but she felt there was something missing in people's lives these days, so she opened a tearoom.

Jo Medycki: *"When I was a little girl or a young married woman, people came to visit us. They came just to have a cup of coffee and a piece of cake, and if you didn't have that, you had cinnamon toast and tea. We had a little party, and everyone would visit and have a good time. But now they're so busy running to the shopping malls they haven't got time to come and visit you. So I decided, well, this (a tearoom) will be nice; people will come and they will sit and they will visit."*

And while they visit the Little Women's Tea Room, Jo and her daughter, Adore, and granddaughter Aimee serve them tea in antique pots and cups, and a triple-tiered tray of treats.

Jo: *"I like the fancy things. My mother always said I had a white thumb."*

Fancy things like an endless variety of mini-sandwiches filled with lobster, or asparagus, or strawberry cream cheese, or spiced cucumbers—or Jo's famous carrot salad marinated in cherry and orange juice. Each tray is laden with numerous bite-size pastries. One month, tiny cupcakes were decorated like Easter baskets. The scones, shaped like bunny rabbits and chicks, were served with real English clotted cream and lemon curd and orange butter.

During one period, Jo, Adore, and Aimee dressed as characters from the Mad Hatter's tea party in *Alice in Wonderland*.

Jim Connell (customer): *"We've had tea in Vienna, we've had tea in most of the European capitals, and I would say that Ellington tops them all."*

Adore Dent: *"We're not just serving tea, we're giving somebody a little pleasure, a little afternoon pleasure, and today with so much stress and people are rushed, we give them the time to sit back and relax."*

The entire tea service is meant to give you pleasure, even when they bring the check. It comes tucked inside *The Book of Tea*. Open it and find a parting thought: "If you are warm, tea will cool you: if you are cold, tea will warm you; if you are sad, tea will cheer you." But maybe it's not the tea.

Maybe it's Jo.

Jo: *"They keep coming back and they make appointment after appointment, the same people. So they're enjoying it, and they love it, and we understand. We have a lot of people that are depressed or ill and they leave here happy. So, that's kind of nice. I cheer 'em up."*

Jo laughs and says, *"Sometimes I wish they wouldn't come back. Then I wouldn't have to invent so many new sandwiches."*

The Little Women's Tea Room in Ellington, for an afternoon's repast that's positively Connecticut. 🍃

FOLLOW-UP:

Although Jo has turned seventy-eight, she has no intention of retiring. She and Adore now hold "theme teas" on Saturdays twice a month that feature storytelling, songs, and poetry. Themes are never repeated and have ranged from "Buttons and Beaus" and "Victorian Skaters" to "Scarlett O'Hara" and "Mark Twain." Many guests now don antique hats when they enter the tearoom—hats collected and decorated by Jo and Adore, who also operate the antiques shop across the hall called Little Women's Attic Treasures. The tearoom and antiques shop are located in a house on the Ellington green that dates to 1790.

Men are sometimes intimidated by what they think of as the female ritual of taking tea. But Jo tries to make them feel comfortable—in part by making larger tea sandwiches for their bigger hands.

Soda Pop

There was a time when small soda bottling plants were common in Connecticut. Now they are difficult to find. But one family is in its third generation of soda making—though the pop isn't delivered by horse and wagon anymore.

The Coke commercial stars Elton John and Paula Abdul, singing "just one reason . . . just one reason . . . just for the taste of it . . . Diet Coke!" Vanna White appears in a close-up, saying, "Sorry, Pepsi, I'm taking this one for a spin."

Cut to a close-up of Bill Bonney, holding up a bottle of Avery's soda and saying, "By making a quality product and selling it for a good price, we know that the people will continue to come back."

Move over, Pepsi. So long, Coke. Look out for Avery's. It's the soft drink that made New Britain famous.

Sherman Avery started making it in 1904. Bill Bonney's dad worked for Avery, then bought the small bottling company when he came home from the war in 1945. Twenty years later, Bill Jr. wanted to buy the place, but couldn't get the refillable bottles he needed.

Bill: *"There's no way we can make a profit if we have a throwaway bottle. The cost of the* *bottle has to be built into the price of the soda."*

The company went to someone else. But Bill eventually bought it back, and he's still making soda pop the old-fashioned way, mixing cane sugar and well water to form syrup, then stirring in the flavor extract. Downstairs the washer scrubs each bottle, and as they march by on a conveyor belt, Bill lightly strikes each one with a ring on his finger. He's listening for cracks. If there's a thud, rather than a ringing sound, it means the bottle is damaged, so it's thrown away. Some of these bottles have been around as long as Bill has.

The bottling machine squirts in the syrup, then the carbonated water, then pops a cap on. That's when Bob Sullivan gets his hands on the bottles. To demonstrate, he grabs a bottle by its neck and flips it once upside down to make sure all the extract mixes in.

Avery's is still located in a turn-of-the-century red barn, where it has always been, right smack in the middle of a residential neighborhood. Bill knows the secret of its success.

Bill: *"We have our own little niche. We make a quality product and we cater to the people. We carry the cases of soda out to the car."*

And all for less than the price of the big guys, like Coke and Pepsi. Chuck Urban of Suffield is a regular customer.

Chuck: *"I like to go into small family-run businesses and buy things, rather than the big supermarkets . . . especially when the product is this good."*

So for sodas like Lime Rickey, Fruit Punch, Pineapple, and Birch Beer, just follow the slogan on the side of the case: "Always Ask for Avery's." It's positively Connecticut. 🖋

MORE ABOUT AVERY'S:

At its peak Avery's was producing forty-five thousand cases of soda a year. But the convenience of supermarket shopping and the rise in health consciousness both hurt the business. As more women went to work, they wanted to do all their marketing in one place, and cut out the trips to Avery's for soda pop. Soda production dropped to about twenty thousand cases a year.

Bill's son, Craig, who joined the business full time after graduating from high school, says they are surviving by distributing spring water, too. The Bonneys have teamed up with another small family business, Village Springs, which bottles spring water directly from the source in Willington, Connecticut. Craig says he hopes Avery's will be around another hundred years. I hope so, too.

Abbott's Lobster in the Rough

NOANK

I always believe that when traveling, you should eat native foods. When in New Orleans, eat gumbo. When in New England, eat lobster. I can't think of anyplace better to eat lobster than Abbott's Lobster in the Rough in Noank. On a warm summer evening, diners tuck away the sweet meat at the point where the river meets the Sound, beneath a sky that turns from blue to cantaloupe, to lilac, then fills with stars.

Hours ago these lobsters were under the sea. In the next few hours they'll be on plates at Abbott's Lobster in the Rough Restaurant.

They're not bragging, but Abbott's will probably serve more lobster this summer than any other restaurant in New England.

Jerry Mears: *"As of today, I just ran it through the computer and we were cooking our twenty-third ton of lobsters. We are on our thirteenth ton of steamer clams."*

A landmark since 1947, Abbott's was bought a decade ago by Jerry and Ruth Mears after their daughter, Dierdre, worked there.

Dierdre: *"I would come home and complain about the place and they would say, 'You know, it's not that bad. It has potential.'"*

There can be up to twenty thousand lobsters at a time in the holding pound, with gallons of seawater constantly being pumped through. All the lobsters are locally caught. You can order ones as big as eight pounds. Jerry once freed a twenty-one-pounder after polling his guests.

If you know some New Englanders who have moved away and are pining for lobster, Abbott's can accomodate you. Their lobsters can be shipped anywhere overnight in the continental United States.

Diane: *"And they will arrive alive?"*

Jerry: *"You bet, full of vim and vigor and ready to go."*

Too bad they can't ship the view. You'd be hard-pressed to find a prettier spot on the Connecticut coastline.

John Otterness (from San Pedro, California): *"I think I'd come anyway just because of the food. But when you add the food to the setting, to all the boats out there, I'm perfectly content to be here forever."*

From here at the mouth of the Mystic River you can see Mason Island in Connecticut, Watch Hill in Rhode Island, and Fisher's Island in New York. Fleets of boats sail by, including antiques from Mystic Seaport. Time it right and you can watch the sun set and the moon rise.

Abbott's Lobster in the Rough, a summer place that's positively Connecticut. ✒

SINCE OUR STORY:

In the winter when Abbott's is closed, you might think Jerry and Ruth Mears would head for the mountains for a change of pace. But they winter in Florida, where Jerry delights in fishing for pompano, which Ruth prepares for dinner.

Dierdre now manages Abbott's, while Jerry and Ruth have opened another restaurant, Costello's, about one hundred yards away in the Noank Shipyard, serving fried seafood.

Abbott's lobsters are cooked under pressure by live steam in a special chamber developed by Ernie Abbott, the original owner. The Mearses use Ernie's original chowder recipe, developed fifty years ago. The clear broth chowder has been featured by food writers from as far as away as London and Paris.

Gourmet Diner

MIDDLETOWN

I'd passed O'Rourke's hundreds of times. It's a little aluminum shoebox of a place, the classic American diner. I have to confess that it wasn't until Gourmet *magazine discovered O'Rourke's that I ventured inside.*

O'Rourke's silver diner has been tucked away at the end of Middletown's Main Street since 1946. Inside, the scent of potatoes frying wafts across the well-worn Formica counter.

So far, it sounds pretty much like your standard diner. But if that's the case, why was O'Rourke's featured in Gourmet magazine, one of the most prestigious food publications in the country? Well, if you have to ask that question, you obviously have never eaten there.

One regular tells us: *"This is fabulous food. This is what I get up in the morning for."*

Professor Khachig Tololyan of Wesleyan University is talking and chewing.

Khachig: *"Best breakfast within a one-hundred-mile radius, and a pretty good lunch."*

With testimonials like that, you might say this place is an institution. But don't say it in front of owner and cook Brian O'Rourke. He says institutions never change, and he

changes every day, coming up with delicious new soups and sauces, numbering now in the thousands.

Brian: *"When you start to make a soup you have an idea, and then when you're making it you open the refrigerator and see something that would go good with it. So you throw it in."*

That's how Brian starts with black beans and ends up creating a soup with double-smoked bacon, barley, and Burgundy.

His uncle owned the diner when Brian was a boy, and he worked there as a kid. But things have changed since Brian took over. Although O'Rourke's makes a great chili dog and is famous for its steamed cheeseburgers, there are dozens of dishes you won't find on any other diner menu. Like Brian's "banana-nana deluxe" pancakes, layered with banana cream cheese, topped with banana syrup and homemade banana kiwi jam. Or polenta topped with poached eggs and finished with a black-eyed peas and corn salsa, which he calls "cuisine art."

Brian: *"I don't believe in recipes. It's kind of like being an artist. If you told an artist to paint that church across the street, he's not going to look at another artist's painting and paint it, he is going to paint his own version of it."*

The self-taught chef comes in at 3:00 A.M. to start baking the breads that have made him famous, like focaccia and pretzel bread. Although the hours are long, O'Rourke clearly relishes cooking.

Brian: *"This is it, this is what I've done all my life and this is what I'll do for the rest of my life."*

But his seems a talent that deserves a bigger, grander setting.

Brian: *"This is all I want. If I hit the lottery tomorrow for twenty million dollars I would never make the diner itself any bigger."*

With the innovative spirit that pervades the kitchen, the diner may be the only item on the menu that does stay the same. O'Rourke's is a place for good food that's positively Connecticut.

DINNERTIME

O'Rourke's is usually open only for breakfast and lunch, but once a month Brian offers Dinner at the Diner. It's a prix fixe menu, featuring dishes like lobster ravioli with champagne sauce, and pecan-encrusted salmon over saffron cheddar grits with a honey lime beurre blanc. Brian is working on a cookbook called Superbowls: A Crock of Soup *and teaching cooking classes. At the end of each class the students eat everything Brian has prepared. He admits some of his students are not really interested in learning to cook. They come for the dinner at the end.*

The Burger Birthplace

NEW HAVEN

The name is immortalized in a lyric in a Whiffenpoofs' song: "From the tables down at Morey's, to the place where Louis dwells." Louis' Lunch is a pint-sized eatery with an enormous legacy. It is here, they say, that the hamburger was born.

It started with Ken Lassen's grandfather Louis, whose specialty was the steak sandwich. After trimming the meat, he had scraps left over. So, the story goes, Louis had the idea of grinding up the scraps, shaping them into a patty, and *voilà,* he'd invented the hamburger.

That was at the turn of the century, and the menu hasn't changed much at Louis' except for the addition of the cheeseburger. If you don't count dessert, hamburgers are the only item on the menu. They're ground fresh daily, cooked in antique vertical gas broilers, and served on white-bread toast.

The slogan "Have it your way" may have pushed Burger King to the top of the fast-food heap, but when you eat at Louis' you have it *their* way. You can order tomato and onion, but whatever you do, don't ask for ketchup.

To Ken, ketchup is a culinary insult.

Ken: *"When kids don't like something, what*

do they do? Their folks are insisting on them eating it, so they load it up with ketchup, and they get it down. But we want you to have a treat, instead of a treatment."

One customer standing in line confirms: "You get it their way. If you're lucky you get cheese on it, and tomatoes and onions."

Diane: "Is that okay?"

Customer: "It's fine with me."

But it's more than the hamburgers that pack the house: It's also the atmosphere, according to another customer.

Second Customer: "It's like eating at home. No other restaurant in town do I get as much aggravation as here!"

If it feels like family here, well it is. Working beside his mom and dad, Jeff is the fourth generation of Lassens behind the counter.

Jeff: "It's a family-type place. If you want to get ribbed a lot, come on down."

And while you're there, check out the history embedded in the walls made from bricks of buildings cleared by "urban renewal."

Even the venerable Louis' was displaced, moving from the corner of Temple and George Streets, where it had been located nearly seventy years, to Crown Street in 1975.

But Ken didn't just move the business, he moved the whole building. And that's when he built his monument to the history of New Haven.

Ken: "I started collecting one brick from every business that they tore down, and that is now represented by this wall over here. A lot of tears went into that wall."

And there are bricks donated by his devoted and well-traveled customers.

Ken: "You name it, it's in there. From the Taj Mahal, to the Parthenon, to the Acropolis, to the czar's palace in Leningrad, and all the stops in between."

There's a certain spirit among the regulars at Louis' Lunch. Because of them, this place means more to the Lassens than just making a living selling hamburgers.

Ken: "Meeting so many people, and talking with all of them, it's just a wonderful education day by day."

Maybe that's what makes Louis' Lunch positively Connecticut. 🍴

SINCE OUR STORY:

In a departure from decades of tradition, Louis' Lunch now serves dinner—on Thursday, Friday, and Saturday nights—to accommodate the resurgent theater and night-club crowd. They've also added hot dogs, and potato salad to the menu. The prices are modest, and when Ken is asked how he makes any money on the hamburgers, he uses a line he remembers from his grandfather. "It's the volume. We lose money on every sandwich, but we make up for it in volume."

Heroes with Heart

The Blind Canoeist

BETHEL

Every once in a while I meet a person who just makes me glad to be alive. That's the kind of person Allan Golabek is. Championship water skier, rock climber, sky diver, plumber. Those are some of the words that describe him. But that's just the beginning.

A day on the water—skiing or canoeing—is pretty close to perfect for Allan Golabek.

Allan: *"It's another source of freedom, you know, when you're out there on the water."*

In the workshop behind his house Allan is building a canoe. It's painstaking, precision work, handcrafting a boat from strips of western red cedar.

Allan talks as he works: *"I start off in the middle and make sure I get a nice tight butt joint. Then I feel the edge."*

His hands slide over the hull he is piecing together.

Allan: *"I engineered this staple gun so I've got somewhat of a guide, so I'll know where I am."*

Allan relies on touch, because he is totally blind, the result of a motorcycle crash four years ago that nearly killed him.

Allan: *"Yeah, I'm lucky to be here. I had two cardiac arrests, ruptured my aorta, had a lot of bone damage. They kind of more or less rebuilt me."*

But it was up to Allan to rebuild his life. The Bethel Lions Club raised $10,000 to help pay his bills and get him a guide dog. But Allan's blindness sent him into a deep depression.

Allan: *"I was so down in the hole that there was no other way out. The only way for me to go was to go to the top. I was able to start climbing that ladder and getting out of that hole."*

The climb started when a friend asked Allan for help building a canoe. At first he said no, asking his buddy, "what use would I be?" But his friend persisted.

Allan: *"As I was helping him out I was feeling around and I said, 'You know, I can do something like this. This is something right up my alley.'"*

As Allan put together a boat of his own, his life started to come together too.

Allan: *"I said okay, this is what happened to me. I gotta deal with this. And before you know it, I said to myself, 'Okay if I'm gonna be blind, I'm gonna be the best blind man out there.'"*

The first canoe Allan built was so special to him that he named her *Cathy Ann* for the ex-girlfriend who helped him recover after his accident. It's hard, but Allan is letting go of the *Cathy Ann,* donating the canoe to the Lions. He's hoping it will raise $10,000 in a raffle to support their good works. After all, the club raised $10,000 for him when he needed it.

Allan's now a member of the club, helping them help others. You see, Allan lost his sight, but his vision is positively Connecticut.

P.S.:

When I met Allan it had been a few years since he lost his sight, so he hadn't been able to watch the TV news for a long time. He'd heard it but he hadn't seen it. He couldn't remember what I looked like. When we arrived and he heard my voice, he said he could picture me immediately. But I still wasn't so sure. He asked me to describe myself. And so, to this day, Allan Golabek thinks I look just like Julia Roberts, only better.

A FURTHER UPDATE:

The Cathy Ann *raffle raised $13,000 for the Lions. The woman who won the canoe gave it back to Allan. He donated the canoe to Guiding Eyes for the Blind, the agency that trained his guide dog, Kessler.*

Cathy Ann will be raffled off again, as a fund-raiser for Guiding Eyes.

The Toyman

I can't remember when I stopped believing in Santa Claus, but I remember when I started again. It was the day I met Eric Hultgren of Westport, also known as the toyman.

At seventy-four years old, Eric Hultgren is still playing a real-life Santa Claus, delivering his beautifully crafted wooden toys to the sick children at Bridgeport Hospital.

"Do you like fishing?" Eric asks as he gives a toy to a child. "This is a bluefish."

Eric's toys are a product of love—his love for his wife of forty-eight years, Shirley. Several years ago she was diagnosed with lung cancer, but by the time doctors discovered the disease, it was too late to operate.

Eric was desperate to save her life.

Eric: *"I'm gonna do something to help other people," he thought, "and maybe the Lord will help us. But it didn't work out."*

Or maybe it did. Shirley died, but the toy-making she inspired became a way for Eric to work through his grief. And it also became a reason for him to get well after he underwent quintuple bypass surgery and then a bout with prostate cancer.

Eric kept on going because of the kids—and the toys.

Eric's father had made a wooden truck for

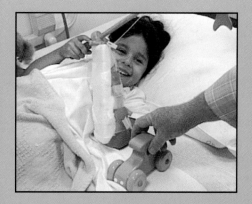

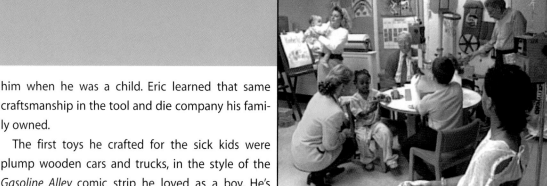

him when he was a child. Eric learned that same craftsmanship in the tool and die company his family owned.

The first toys he crafted for the sick kids were plump wooden cars and trucks, in the style of the *Gasoline Alley* comic strip he loved as a boy. He's invented some toys specifically for children confined to a hospital bed, like a fishing pole, which he demonstrated to a small patient, showing him how to reel in a wooden fish over his hospital tray table.

Our first story on Eric aired nationwide on *Good Morning America*. After that came articles by *The New York Times, Parade* magazine, and the Associated Press. *Creative Woodworks* magazine called him "the legendary toyman."

ABC's *World News Tonight* named Eric its Person of the Week.

This is what Forrest Sawyer said about Eric, in that broadcast.

Forrest Sawyer: *"The person we choose this week can teach us all a lesson in how learning to help ourselves can go a long way in helping others as well."*

That first story was the beginning of a flood of mail—more than eight thousand letters, which Eric answered individually. Some contained money to buy materials for toys. But Eric is still using his pension and Social Security for that.

Eric: *"If I were to take the money for it, then I would lose the kick of giving it away."*

Instead Eric plans to use the $7,000 in donations as seed money for a special project. He'd like to publish a pamphlet about his toys and the joy they've brought to the children in the hospital, then mail one to each person who has written to him, appealing to them to help him raise money to build a new children's wing at the hospital.

MORE ABOUT THIS STORY:

Our segment on Eric aired on national TV after ABC asked its affiliated stations to submit stories that embodied something special about their area. Eric's story was chosen as one of five from around the country. That led to lots of media attention and donations from around the nation. Eric approached the Bridgeport Hospital Foundation about creating a fund to rebuild the pediatric ward—and in spring of 1998 the new ward opened. It's brighter and more spacious, with rooms that can accommodate little patients and their families, who can spend the night. In keeping with the spirit of one of the hospital's founders, P. T. Barnum, the twenty-two-bed unit has a circus theme.

And Eric's good work is spreading. Woodworkers are using his diagrams to make toys for sick kids in hospitals from Seattle to Philadelphia.

No wonder he sometimes finds himself thinking: "It's a great life."

He says that in spite of his latest setback.

Eric: *"Last September I was so healthy it was unbelievable, and I figured that I had beat the cancer. Then in February I got this funny backache, and I thought, is it just old age or is it me being bent over the workbench?"*

Unfortunately it wasn't either of those things, and Eric is now battling cancer of the spine, undergoing chemotherapy. And through it all, he still thinks of his beloved Shirley.

Eric: *"I miss her. I dream about her once in a while. The only thing is, she never talks to me in the dream."*

Diane: *"If she could talk to you, what would she say about all this?"*

Eric: *"She'd say 'You're making a mess. You'd better finish one thing before you start something else.'"*

No, Eric, I think she'd say "Good job, keep it up, Dear." Because Eric Huttgren is bringing happiness to children that's positively Connecticut.

You can contact the toyman by writing:
Eric Hultgren
94 Clapboard Hill Road
Westport, CT 06880

Aboard the Eagle

NEW LONDON

When the Special Olympics World Games came to Connecticut, I had the chance of a lifetime. The Coast Guard's historic training vessel, the barque Eagle, led an international parade of tall ships in New Haven Harbor. I managed to get on board for two glorious days.

On board the *Eagle*, cameraman R. J. Tattersall and I are not the only new recruits. Besides two special Olympians and their coaches, a new crop of cadets is boarding their floating classroom today for the summer.

A tour by boatswain's mate Carl Schultz, helps us get oriented on the 297-foot-long barque. Built in 1936 by the Germans, it takes a lot of muscle power to sail the *Eagle*.

Carl is at the wheel—actually three wheels yoked together.

Carl: *"To control the rudder you just haul like a big dog because there's no hydraulics involved."*

There's a big crew on board, sixty enlisted personnel and officers and one hundred cadets. The cadets are hard at work polishing the brass until you can see the reflection of the mast shining in the compass housing. Captain Donald Grosse invites me to dinner with a few other guests in his flag cabin, the only part of the ship that remains the way it was when Hitler commanded the German Navy.

Captain Grosse: *"We always like to say that Adolph slept here. We don't know if he ever was on board overnight, but if he was, that's where he slept."*

At 6:00 P.M. the horn sounds.

Six cadets, two on each wheel, spin the wheels to turn the rudders. We're under way.

Special Olympics sailors Diane Dahling and Molly King are eager mates.

Diane (to Diane Dahling): *"It's a little harder than raising the sail on your boat."*

Diane D. (with a chuckle): *"Yes."*

Diane: *"When they said 'heave ho,' how did you feel?"*

Molly: *"I said heave, huh? What does that mean?"*

Diane: *"But now you know."*

Molly (smiling broadly): *"Yeah!"*

Diane Dahling's parents, Jan and Gary Lehrman, coach the New London Special Olympics sailing team.

Gary: *"Diane was totally in terror of water. We gradually got her used to it by getting her on boats. But the last two years have been sort of miraculous, because she has taken to sailing and doing things that we never thought she would be able to do."*

One thing Diane is still afraid of—heights. She won't even look up at the masts, rising 150 feet above the deck. But her teammate takes on the cadets' challenge to go aloft.

The cadets cheer as Molly and Jan climb up into the rigging. When they're squarely back on

Susan Saint James

deck, they embrace. Officers and cadets gather round to "high-five" the teenager.

Molly's courage inspires me. It's nearly dusk as I get up my nerve to climb the rigging on a mast rising the equivalent of fifteen stories above the deck. A cadet will accompany me. We don safety belts, with a large hook to attach to the rigging. But as we climb I learn we have to unhook and refasten the belt after each step, so there are moments when no harness will catch us if feet or hands slip. The boat gently rolls with the waves. The rigging is moist with the night air.

At seventy feet, just below the crow's nest, I decide I've had enough, drink in the commanding view, and head back down. As we reach the deck, my guide rates the climb: "The good news is you went at least ten feet higher than Hillary Clinton."

The cadets cheer. I'm now one of them!

In the morning we wake up in New Haven Harbor surrounded by boaters.

Captain Grosse: *"They understand that this ship is a remnant of the age of sail, but it's also something that's bringing the waterfront back to life."*

Pipes sound as dignitaries arrive by launch, led by Senator Edward Kennedy and his sister Eunice Shriver who founded the Special Olympics. Some go aloft, including actress Susan Saint James, a long-time Special Olympics supporter. Congresswoman Rosa DeLauro climbs higher than anyone else, including Olympic gymnast Bart Conner.

The fleet of tall ships from around the globe falls into formation. The *Eagle* leads the proud parade. All too soon we pull up to the pier.

Diane Dahling and Molly King toss a line to a waiting hand on the dock, and a crowd cheers. The Stars and Stripes, flying from the stern, floats in the breeze as a late afternoon sun breaks through the clouds.

Two days on board the *Eagle*, an adventure that was positively Connecticut. ⚓

P.S.:

Talking to Captain Grosse after watching Rosa DeLauro's spectacular climb up into the rigging, I tell him I wish I had climbed higher. "Oh, don't feel bad," he answers, "once you get above forty feet it's all the same." "What do you mean?" I ask. "Oh, anything above forty feet and the fall will kill you," he says, a twinkle in his eye.

The Best Medicine

*I*n 1996 when the Olympic flame made its journey through America to Atlanta, it was carried by "community heroes," people who earned that honor through service to others. One of them is a personal hero of mine, a young man by the name of Philip Licastri.

Since the times of the ancient Greeks, the Olympic torch has been carried by the fleet of foot, the strong of heart, and now by the generous in spirit. Philip Licastri has a generosity without measure. That's why United Way chose Phil to carry the torch.

Denise Cesareo nominated Phil: *"Instantly Phil came to mind, absolutely instantly."*

But the twenty-nine-year-old Westport man would never call himself a hero.

Phil: *"Everything that I do I enjoy so much, it's become a part of what I am."*

Phil is a personal trainer, specializing in clients trying to gain or to regain their health. That makes him a natural for the transformation he makes at Stamford Hospital. There he goes by the name of Doctor Willoughby, MD—not a medical doctor but a doctor of mirth, who comes to spread cheer.

Phil: *"Very few people have an opportunity to go and make somebody else's life easier,* *especially when some of the people who are in the situation may be going through one of the hardest times of their life."*

At least twice a month Doctor Willoughby sees patients at the hospital, walking from one room to the next in his gigantic red shoes. In one room, Phil twists a balloon into a crown and places it gently on the head of an elderly woman who is sitting in a chair, breathing with the help of an oxygen tube. She's delighted by his humor, and by his kindness.

Phil: *"To see them smile really makes you feel special, makes you feel happy as well."*

Phil *is* special. Just ask any of the seniors at Eldercare, a daycare center for seniors in Norwalk.

Dora Scaglia: *"Phil is a wonderful boy. He'd do anything for you."*

Phil is there at least twice a week to teach an armchair exercise class. He always has a smile, a word of encouragement, and time to listen.

Phil: *"I am emotionally attached to all of them, and I get so much back from them. It's like having fifty or sixty grandparents. I feel like I'm their grandson. I get to laugh and joke with them."*

Legend has it that the sacred Olympic flame symbolizes knowledge and life and that the torch relay signifies the passing of that flame from one generation to the next—something these people say this young man understands very well.

In her nomination of Phil, Eldercare director Denise Cesareo described him as "loving and loyal, with a heart of gold."

Denise: *"He greets every client with a handshake, a kiss, or a hug if they need it. He is just the ambassador of the generations."*

Philip Licastri, a community hero who is positively Connecticut.

FOLLOW-UP:

When Phil met the woman he planned to marry, he took her to Eldercare to meet his surrogate grandparents. When Kathleen enjoyed the visit and asked to go there again, Phil knew he had met the right woman.

Stamford Hospital's HAHA (Health And Humor Association) is an all-volunteer program of about thirty clowns visiting patients. The program was started in 1992 by Penny Smith, who had been exposed to clowning while she was a breast cancer patient at Sloan Kettering Hospital in New York. Penny called on Michael Christenson of the Big Apple Circus, and he helps each new crop of clowns polish their technique.

Senior Savers

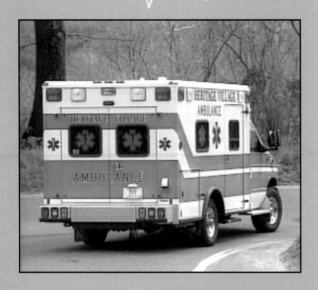

What do you dream about doing after you retire? Playing a little golf? Traveling? Or just relaxing? Some people seek ways to make a difference. They still hear the call that they are needed by the people around them. That's what led some retirees in Southbury to start their own ambulance corps. They believe it is the only one in the nation operated entirely by senior citizens.

When the crew on this ambulance races an elderly man to Danbury Hospital with a possible heart attack, they understand.

Art Bosley: "We can relate to them better than anybody else. We are all in the same boat. Most of the people are very sympathetic to the patients."

That is because each of the seventy members of the ambulance corps is a senior citizen. They live in Heritage Village, a retirement community of more than four thousand people in Southbury.

Some of the volunteers are certified emergency medical technicians. Most have had no previous medical experience.

Chris Carter, president of the association, had a personal reason for joining.

Chris: "On the twenty-ninth of September 1989 my husband had a heart attack. The first *people who came were security, and then the Heritage Village ambulance."*

She soon joined the squad. Another member recruited Ruth Schoenfeld.

Ruth: *"I figured that it would be time to give something back to my fellow neighbors, and we are the most sympathetic people. Care givers, you will find, have a sixth sense. They know what to say at the right time. It just comes with wanting to care for people."*

The squad celebrated its twenty-fifth anniversary last year by buying a new ambulance, with $85,000 the members raised themselves.

The crew on the ambulance must meet certain physical requirements, mainly strength and mobility.

Art Bosley: *"Lifting is the biggest problem that we definitely have, and that is why we have tried to gear ourselves with the most modern equipment, so that we do very little lifting."*

The new ambulance is outfitted with special steps and a gurney to minimize lifting.

Fred Broege is an emergency medical technician who was once a patient. When he fainted in the shower, his wife knew who to call.

Fred: *"She called 911, and the next thing that I know there are about ten people in that bathroom."*

Fred says knowing that there is an ambulance service in the village gives everyone peace of mind. And there are other rewards.

Fred: *"When you get to a patient and he has had a heart attack and you can see him dying in front of you, and you start CPR and he passes out and you get him back, and you bring him to the hospital. Saving someone. There is nothing more rewarding than that."*

The Heritage Village Ambulance Association, a team of dedicated volunteers that is positively Connecticut.

P.S.:

Ruth Schoenfeld is on another mission, holding seminars for the public on women and heart disease. Heart trouble is one of the main complaints that has people at the village dialing 911.

Lighthouse Keepers

SHEFFIELD ISLAND

The Connecticut coastline is dotted with lighthouses, but very few can actually be visited. Some of us cruise by them in boats or gaze at them from the shore and wonder what life in one would be like. One Connecticut lighthouse was a family's home for years, but now it has been turned back to us, to treasure and preserve.

On the last weekend in May they arrive on Sheffield Island like a military brigade, aboard vintage military boats. The volunteers from the group known as the Telephone Pioneers are armed with everything from paintbrushes to a backhoe.

Bob Archambault: *"The biggest thing was logistics of getting the people out here, getting the materials, getting the food, because there's no little corner store you can go to for mustard or for nails."*

Divided into squadrons, they mount the two-day campaign. Some work on the long-dormant grape arbor, building a trellis and tying up vines. Others dig trenches and construct a shed to house a generator, bringing the first reliable electricity to the island. Cosmetics count too, from landscaping to painting.

A woman standing on a ladder is scraping paint from the transom over the main entrance into the lighthouse: *"The salt air really eats at the paint, and this has got many years of layers on here, so I'm scraping it off."*

Salt air has been eating away at paint here since the lighthouse was built in 1868. A working light for forty years, its kerosene beacon was replaced by an automated lighthouse on Green's Ledge in 1902. Ten years later a family bought the sixty-five-acre island, according to a local historian.

Bill Sculley: *"They not only had their own gardens, but also their own livestock on the island. In fact at one time much of the island was under cultivation, and seasonally livestock were swum to the island from the mainland to graze on pasturelands."*

The pastures are gone now, replaced by the wooded bird sanctuary that takes up most of the island. The lighthouse is now owned by the Norwalk Seaport Association, which bought it to help save the island from condominium development.

Part of the Telephone Pioneers' job, fixing up the caretaker's cottage, includes installing a kitchen. Louis Devizia worked on that.

Louis: *"Nothing was square, plumb, or level, but it worked out good."*

The Pioneers' restoration project helped the Seaport Association get one step closer to its goal for the island. They'd eventually like the lighthouse to become a museum, a monument to Norwalk's past and its heyday as a shipping port.

Looking through the lens in the lighthouse, you'll see they've already preserved the view from the tower fifty-five feet above Sheffield's rocky beach.

Divers are still recovering the wreckage of ships that failed to heed the lighthouse warning, and visitors are still discovering the history and beauty of Sheffield Island and its lighthouse. The enthusiasm and elbow grease of the Telephone Pioneers are helping preserve a part of the past that's positively Connecticut.

UPDATE:

About a year after our story, a hurricane ripped up plantings and eroded the beaches. The Pioneers returned to repair the damage. In 1998 the Seaport Association called on the Pioneers again, this time to put in an environmental toilet, a kiosk, and a walking trail through the McKinney Wildlife Refuge, which shares the island. Federal grant money pays for some of the work, but there is a string attached. The dollars must be matched by volunteer labor. Sheffield Island Lighthouse is one of only a few lighthouses left in the region that people can get into and explore. The island is now available for corporate events and clam-bakes, and eventually the Seaport hopes to offer docent-guided tours.

Christmas Village

TORRINGTON

S ome people don't appreciate how much civil servants care about their jobs and the people they serve. But spend one December afternoon with Parks Department workers in Torrington and you'll get a pretty good idea. Every December for fifty years they have created Christmas Village. They put a great deal of care and ingenuity into the display, and their reward is the joy of the little ones who troop through.

For two weeks before Christmas, Santa takes up residence in Torrington. So far from the North Pole, you say? Oh, he doesn't come alone. St. Nick brings a few of his elves, and a herd of reindeer too.

And he has helpers who get the Christmas Village ready for his annual visit—helpers like Gus Lucia, a Parks Department worker.

Gus: *"I look forward to this all year long."*
Diane: *"You do?"*
Gus: *"Yeah. Christmas is my favorite time of year."*

Gus Lucia decorates the elves' workshop from top to bottom with toys. He works a little magic, too, rewiring battery-operated toys and then hiding control wires in a secret panel. He likes to surprise the little visitors.

**MORE ABOUT
THIS STORY:**

Gus: *"You can kind of play around if they're looking at something that's not moving and you start that moving. Their eyes light up, they jump, they scream, and everybody has a good time."*

When Gus looks at these children, he remembers coming here as a little boy.

Gus: *"Being as little as I was, I thought it was a big town and a magical village."*

His coworker Jim Sica recalls: *"waiting in line with my feet freezing, because they used to have mobs of people here."*

They still do. Twenty thousand people visit over two weeks. Each child has a chance to sit on Santa's knee and take home a present.

Diane (to Santa): *"Have they been good boys and girls this year?"*

Santa: *"Oh, yes, bad boys won't come to see Santa."*

Jim decks out Santa's throne room with more decorations than you can count. He loves watching the kids tell Santa their Christmas wishes.

Jim: *"Some of them are scared and they cry and holler. Some are in awe, they don't say much."*

When they grow up, many of them bring their own children.

Lori Binstadt: *"It makes Christmas really special for the kids. It feels like you are really at Santa's village and the North Pole."*

Diane (to three-year-old Evan Fedorovich): *"What did you think of Santa's house?"*

Evan: *"Pretty good."*

Julie Fedorovich (his mom): *"Pretty good, or really good?"*

Evan (reconsidering): *"Really good!"*

If you visit on a weekend, be prepared to stand in line. Some people tell us that's part of the fun. They visit with their neighbors and sip free hot chocolate.

Santa is in Torrington till Christmas eve, but his spirit lingers through the season in the hearts of his helpers, who are positively Connecticut. 🎵

In 1997 Torrington marked the fiftieth anniversary of Christmas Village with a celebration that re-created the 1947 opening of the village. A 250-year-old stagecoach piled high with gifts transported Santa to the village, where he was met with a kiss from Mrs. Claus and a cheer from the Torrington High School cheerleaders. A thousand people turned out including Olga Buzinski, the widow of Carl Buzinski, who founded Christmas Village based on the plans he made while confined to a sanitarium for treatment of tuberculosis. The village costs Torrington about $30,000 each year, including electricity, police overtime, and reindeer rental. But even in this age of municipal cost-cutting, the village hasn't suffered. Why not? Parks Director Craig Schroeder says: "Because it's part of Torrington's memory."

LEAP of Faith

While most students at Yale Law School were busy enough cracking the books, one was looking at the community outside the walls of ivy and was determined to make it better. You might say Henry Fernandez took a LEAP of faith.

On the graffiti-marked basketball courts at New Haven's Church Street South housing project, there are lots of kids with hoop dreams—hoping against the odds that the game will be their ticket out of poverty.

But these kids have a better shot, after spending their summer in the LEAP program. Fourteen-year-old Robert Baskin explains why he signed up.

Robert: *"I just thought of coming to LEAP because I'm off the streets, I'm not doing nothing bad, and I'm being positive."*

LEAP stands for Leadership, Education, and Athletics in Partnership. That translates into giving opportunities, socially and academically, to inner-city kids seven to fourteen years old.

Henry Fernandez founded LEAP while still in Yale Law School, and in the last four years has helped it grow. It involves more than 1,000 children a year in New Haven, Hartford, and New London.

Henry: *"If as Americans we hope to be a moral people, then we have to say these are our children, not just the ones that we gave birth to or that we're fortunate enough to be related to, but that each of these children is ours and in each of them we see a piece of ourselves. If we can't do that we've lost a good part of who we are as Americans."*

LEAP's storefront classroom is filled with young African American kids at computers. They are learning from LEAP counselors—high school and college students who come from backgrounds just like theirs. Kids like them; kids who are making it.

Henry has a dream.

Henry: *"Sometime in the future we won't always have to think that we're in a crisis, but we'll have young people who develop into older people who become leaders, mayors, teachers, parents who go about raising children, their own and others."*

In the summer, LEAP counselors live in the projects as full-time role models for their students. In some cases they fill the gap left by a missing parent.

One summer the kids traveled to the South, following the footsteps of the Freedom Riders, the civil rights activists who changed America.

For counselor al-Rahim Williams it was a chance to see where history was made and to share the experience with his students.

Al-Rahim: *"I was excited, and if I'm excited I know they're gonna be excited. Enthusiasm is contagious."*

As director of LEAP, Henry Fernandez has seen much of what's bad for kids—abuse, neglect, the ravages of poverty.

Henry: *"But I also get to see the people everyday who fight against that, who say, 'I'm going to stand for this child.'"*

For his work, twenty-eight-year-old Fernandez has been nationally recognized by MTV and *Mademoiselle* magazine, picked as one of ten civic leaders making a difference in their communities.

Henry Fernandez: a young community leader to watch, who's positively Connecticut. 🎗

UPDATE:

Henry left LEAP to take a fellowship at Yale, thinking and writing about issues facing urban schools. In his final year he oversaw the opening of a large community center in New Haven and the establishment of a program that provides a transition for LEAP kids who want to be LEAP counselors.

Of course LEAP doesn't begin and end with Henry Fernandez. He founded LEAP with the help of a woman whose family has been in New Haven for generations. Ann Calabrese saw the dramatic separation between people who lived in different neighborhoods in the same city. She realized that some kids needed a mentor, someone like them, who had chosen education as the way to a better life. In the New Haven area there are thousands of potential mentors attending Yale, Southern Connecticut State University, the University of New Haven, and other colleges. These mentors take on a "family" of kids and help them learn to communicate, negotiate, and settle problems without violence. It's an extraordinary lesson in commitment to community and, for the children, a chance to believe that their lives are worth something.

Spirit of the Drums

NORTH BRANFORD

This is not just a story about drums and fifes. It's about friendship and fellowship and family. The year 1933 was a good time to start up the North Branford Fife and Drum Corps. The boys were eight to fourteen years old.

Wally Fulton: *"During the Depression, drum corps was the only hobby there was around. There was no Little League, no mini-basketball, and all that stuff. If you were in a drum corps, you got to get on a school bus and get out of town. If you weren't in a drum corps, you stayed in town."*

And it seemed as if every time they left town, they came home with trophies and medals.

Bob Redican: *"Every year was a heyday for this corps. This corps set a lot of high precedents in the competitive field of ancient fifing and drumming."*

Ralph Marrone: *"Two years in a row we were picked as the top drum corps in all classes."*

In 1939 the World's Fair put these country boys and their small town on the map.

Anthony Daly: *"We had to go from the New York City YMCA out to the fairgrounds (in Queens) via subway, carrying bass drums and snare drums."*

Ralph Marrone: *"It was an awesome event really. There were just so many people from all over, and here we were just a bunch of people from out in the country, and competing against a good number of people."*

Before thousands of spectators, the North Branford Corps was named world champion.

During World War II, the corps shrank when twenty-four members went into the service. One was killed in action. The rest came home, but raising their families took precedence over marching, and the members drifted apart. But as their kids grew up, these cousins and brothers and pals came back together. They were hooked.

It was the music, and more.

According to Curly Provenzano it was "the love of fellowship, because we grew up together."

Diane: *"To be able to keep friends as long as this, is really an extraordinary thing in the world that we live in today."*

Anthony Daly: *"Don't you think that's what's wrong with the world? There's not enough people that are friends?"*

Luke Camarota: *"We always hung around together, we played together, we did everything together. We never had a problem."*

Diane: *"Never? No fights? Ever?"*

Luke: *"Naaaah, we used to argue a little bit, but…"*

Another corp member speaks up: *"Him and I fought."* Everyone laughs.

Maybe they don't step as smartly as before, and there's some arthritis in the fingers that twirl the drumsticks, but watch the crowd as the North Branford Fife and Drum Corps marches by. You'll see that the music still makes hearts pound and feet tap. The corps makes the local Memorial Day parade an event that's positively Connecticut. ♪

MORE ABOUT THIS STORY:

In 1998 the North Branford Fife and Drum Corps celebrated the tenth anniversary of its reorganization. Six charter members—all in their seventies—are still active. One of them is Ralph Colter, whose father, Earl, organized the corps.

In September 1939, the month after the corps won top honors at the World's Fair, a reporter for the New Haven Register wrote this: "Perfect coordination combined with the splendid bearing of the corps makes a lasting impression on the visitor. After playing several old favorites such as 'Grandfather's Clock,' 'Hail, Hail,' and 'Whistler and His Dog,' the corps begins to drill up and down the driveway. Soon they march out to the athletic club field. Seeing and hearing these boys marching in the dusk cannot help but bring to mind the almost identical corps which practiced in various communities in New England more than 150 years ago. One can almost imagine a British redcoat sneaking up behind."

About the Author

Diane Smith has been a news anchor and reporter at WTNH News Channel 8 in New Haven, Connecticut, for over fifteen years. She is the correspondent for *Positively Connecticut*, a weekly feature that searches out the inspiring, warm, funny, and sometimes downright strange stories that give Connecticut its character.

Diane's news reporting has earned her an Emmy Award. Her public affairs documentaries have earned state and national awards from the Associated Press, the Society of Professional Journalists, the National Commission against Drunk Driving, and other organizations. She has been honored by the American Cancer Society for the News Channel 8 campaign to educate women about breast cancer.

Born in Newark, New Jersey, Diane lives on the Connecticut shoreline with her husband, Tom Woodruff, and her dogs Chancellor and Chester.